WHAT PEOPLE ARE SAYING ABOUT
LOVE GOD MAKE MONEY

"Mike Moore writes helpfully and winsomely about one of the most challenging issues for marketplace Christians: How do I live my faith in the workplace? He's built a successful business and made some of the personal mistakes that came with that experience, which puts him in a position to share how our mistakes make us more credible to those who are watching. His vulnerability is a real plus here as the confident businessman meets the servant and produces a helpful approach to realizing God's plan for me to live my faith."

—Jamie Bush
Principal, Bush and Company, Boston, MA

"Love God Make Money reveals the multiple ways to acknowledge GOD in our businesses. Mike Moore's unique ability to explain complex truths using simple day-to-day illustrations will assist any businessperson who seeks a deeper level of the 'why' behind the 'what' in doing business. This follow-up book to Love God Hate Church is a MUST-read for ANYONE in the business community!"

—Bill Noble
William Noble Rare Jewels
Highland Park, Dallas, TX

"Walking your faith in the workplace isn't always easy. Mike Moore shows you how in this deeply spiritual—and incredibly entertaining—new book."

—Michael Levin
New York Times best selling author

"Mike Moore tackles the age-old conflict for the follower of Jesus: How do I pursue career and financial excellence without compromising my humility to and dependence on God? His passion is to unlock the keys to God's wisdom, because wisdom brings riches, honor, long life, and health. Thanks, Mike, for sharing your passion for doing life God's way, and helping others to do the same!"

—**Randy Hammon, Author of**
The Safe Money System & Religion vs. Relationship: Discovering the God I Always Knew Was There!

"In the sea of books about dreams, goals, and success, Love God Make Money stands out. These pages present a refreshing portrait of God's kind of success. Each chapter grips the reader with a beautiful blend of powerful truths communicated with boldness, clarity, and conviction. I experienced many "aha moments" as Mike Moore skillfully weaves real-life stories to illustrate each insight. Seldom have I read a book in one sitting, but Love God Make Money kept me hooked on lessons that have the power to transform. When the last chapter ends, the reader cannot help but go back and revisit the powerfully relevant and life-changing truths."

—**Janet Perez Eckles**
Author and International Speaker

"*Love God Make Money* is a down-to-earth guide on how to allow your spiritual being to influence your daily business dealings. Using examples from his life's interactions, Mike Moore describes our relationships and how we view them—from our own view, from someone's else view, and from God's viewpoint. This weaves a compelling story that will inspire even the most lost soul to a richer and happier life. And it reminds you that the wealthiest person in the world is not the one who has the most, but the one who needs the least. It is the kind of book you will not put down and will read again and again."

—David S. Ellis, MD
Dallas, TX

"*Mike is a unique mix of businessman, pastor, and friend. I have had the privilege of being on the receiving end of his outlandish hospitality, unconditional love, and bear hugs. He is the best person to show you that you don't have to compromise values, personal holiness, and your value for people to be successful in the marketplace. This book will show you that if we want to honor the God we keep professing about, we must honor our gift.*"

—Lijo Mathew
Founder, Slingshot Holding
Dubai, United Arab Emirates

"*Mike Moore has done it again. His "Love God" series is imparting God's heart to the neglected, unseen, and misunderstood. Love God Make Money is a long-overdue message for Christians in the marketplace. Mike's forty-plus years of extravagant generosity and hospitality to anyone and everyone has transformed thousands of lives. He has proven that marketplace leaders don't just garner resources for the kingdom; they are frontline agents extending God's kingdom outside the church walls. Mike has lived the pages in this book and is proof that you can make money and love God well."*

—Michael Miller
Senior Pastor of the Upper Room
Dallas, TX

Love God
Make Money

♥ | 💰

Love God Make Money

BUSINESS AND GOD ARE NOT ENEMIES

MIKE MOORE

For more information, contact:
www.mikemooreonline.com

Paperback: 978-1-947368-00-2
eBook: 978-1-947368-01-9

Library of Congress Control Number: 2017945210

This book is dedicated to a lot of people, known and unknown. Business assistants, support staff, store clerks, coffee-shop baristas, coaches, mentors, family, friends, even strangers—thousands of people who have helped me get where I am today in my life and career. And they all have been gifts from God!

Contents

Introduction

A MUST-READ

Hi, I'm Mike Moore, a businessman in Dallas and someone continually striving to become a "master in the art of living!"

I like the way L. P. Jacks defined it in the early twentieth century:

> A master in the art of living makes no distinction between his work and his play; his labor and his leisure; his mind and his body; his education and his recreation. He hardly knows which is which. He simply pursues his vision of excellence in whatever he is doing, and leaves others to determine whether he is working or playing. Because to himself, he always appears to be doing both.

That is living life to the fullest. If our work does not have an element of play for us, why do it in the first place? And whether we believe it or not, God owns the organizations we work for and our individual work. So why not enjoy it with Him?

As a businessman, I like to work, close deals, engage with people, and earn money. This notion of God first, family second, business third, and fun last? I don't buy it!

This doesn't mean you have to talk about God for eight hours while the company pays you to get a job done. But it does mean acknowledging God in whatever you are doing. We all can do this. The wisest man ever to live was King Solomon. He said, "Trust in the Lord with all your heart, and do not rely on your own understanding. Acknowledge God in all your ways, and He will make straight your paths." So, what does it mean to acknowledge God in all we do? In all our daily work or business?

It can be something as small as, "God, as I walk into this business meeting, I want to acknowledge the fact that you are here and you are with me—whether I feel it or not." Acknowledge his presence in your life no matter what you are doing, just like your son would acknowledge that you are his daddy or mommy, no matter where he happened to be.

When we make God into a set of religious rules and regulations, we can only compare what we do with what we believe He is telling us to do. But if our Heavenly Father is deeply concerned about our every thought, feeling, and action—if we know His deep love for us— then we can go with Him as we pursue being our best.

God has been left out of our businesses for so long that we are beginning to believe that God and business are enemies, opposites, antonyms. But when I see the hustle and bustle of large cities like New York, Rome, Singapore, or Tokyo, I can't help but wonder how active Heaven must be. I can't imagine the hustle and bustle of the organization that God manages. If the earth is the Lord's, and all it contains and those who dwell on it, can you imagine all the activity in Heaven?

This book is about acknowledging God in our lives, especially in our daily work and business. Why? Because that is where many men and women find their value and significance. I heard a wealthy investment banker say, "Money is the adult scorecard. Whoever dies with the most toys, wins."

I do not agree with that statement. Instead, money is a gift from God. The more you make, the more you are able to give away to help others. And the more you make, the more you are able to enjoy for yourself and your family! It is all His anyway! All those who die knowing they used their money to help others—family, friends, or those less fortunate—they are the ones who win.

Consider what Paul said about Jesus Christ: "For you know the grace of our Lord Jesus Christ, that though He was *rich*, yet for your sake *He became poor*, so that you through His poverty might become *rich*" (2 Corinthians 8:9 NIV, emphasis added).

Now many "religious people" might assume that's a prosperity gospel: love God and you become a billionaire. Well, some may be billionaires, and some might become millionaires. But is that the only kind of wealth Paul is talking about here?

Jesus, who owns everything, became poor so that we might become rich. Rich in what? Money, houses, and cars? Or love, mercy, and grace? We tend to think of richness as being simply monetary and forget the richness of blessings like family, health, and wealth, like compassion, joy, forgiveness, and peace. At the end of the day, if you know God through Jesus Christ His Son and have been filled with His Spirit, you are already rich!

Therefore, we acknowledge God in all that we do in business because the outcome is in His hands. But that doesn't mean we shouldn't do everything we can to make that outcome a good one. So why not make as much money as your industry allows you to make? Why not be the number one person in your field or at least strive to be? Why not? *Someone* will be. Why not you?

So be the best you can be at what you do, but acknowledge God in how you do it. Take pride in what you do, but don't let it be your scorecard. Keep an attitude of gratefulness and respect for others, and look for ways to encourage rather than blaming, criticizing, or complaining. These are the true riches!

Mike

Part 1

PASSION

♥ | 💰

1

WALK OUT YOUR PASSION

What does it mean to walk out your passion in business? It means living an authentic life in the business world. It means doing what you love with a fire inside you.

But take a look at most of the companies and organizations that exist today, and you won't see people walking out their passions. They're not doing business in a way that inspires their coworkers, bosses, and employees. Most of the time, their colleagues simply put up with them so they can all collect their paychecks, drive home, and watch their favorite TV shows.

What would it be like if conducting business were more like falling in love?

Meet Jonah. Jonah is in love. I'm talking head-over-heels, butterflies-in-the-stomach, fireworks-going-off-like-crazy love. The kind of love most of us feel before we get married.

This describes Jonah to a T. Jonah can't wait to marry Jenny, his longtime girlfriend. He gets her a beautiful diamond ring, pops the question, and she says yes. They get engaged and everybody's excited. Jenny's giddy. Jonah's giddy. He's ready to settle down and spend the rest of his life with this woman. He's made a choice to love her forever. And Jenny—well, she couldn't be more excited. She feels like the man of her dreams came along and is now sweeping her up into a beautiful tomorrow.

Jonah has never particularly loved his job, but after he meets Jenny, he has a new spring in his step. He works at a big company where he meets with a lot of independent vendors. Before he got engaged to Jenny, he was often grumpy when he went out to meet new vendors, but now he's always in a great mood. He's interested in who they are, because he's just so happy! Jonah is no longer judging people, the way he used to. He is so filled with the love he has for Jenny that it changes the way he does business. It actually changes the way he relates to people, because that love is simply overflowing in his heart.

Jonah is walking around on this huge high because of the love he has for Jenny. It changes the way he responds to everything. If he goes into Starbucks and a guy cuts him off in line, he's like, "Go ahead, bro!" He's got so much love in his heart that he can't be offended.

It shines through every one of his daily interactions, and before long, Jonah gets promoted at work because his manager sees what a great job he's doing by getting the vendors to sign. The vendors feel like somebody actually cares about them and their problems. For the first time, they feel valued and genuinely heard.

Jonah's living his passion and it's changing him, changing the way he treats people, transforming the way he does business. But how do the rest of us walk out our passions? Especially those of us who aren't lucky enough to have a Jenny in our lives?

A few months ago, I spoke to two very different groups of people. I spoke to a bunch of twenty-year-olds, and then the next weekend, I spoke to a bunch of fifty-year-olds. The fifty-year-olds were beat up and pressed down by life. They had no dreams. But the twenty-year-olds—all they had were dreams.

"I want to help you get to a place where nobody can squash your dreams," I told them. "I want you to walk out your passion and live it every day. Whether your dreams all come true or not isn't the issue. If you pursue the dream, whether you 'make it' or not, you win, because you've got that all-consuming love driving everything you do."

Of course, you can't speak to a bunch of people about passion without the focus getting turned back on you at some point.

"What are *you* passionate about, Mike?" they asked. "We want to know!"

"You guys really want to know what I'm passionate about?" I replied.

"Yeah, we want to know. You've been talking to us about *our* passions—so what about yours?"

"OK then," I began. "First, I'm going to tell you what I'm *not* passionate about. I'm not passionate about getting up in the morning to follow a bunch of religious regulations. I'm not passionate about believing in a God who tells me I have to follow fifty rules for Him to be OK with me. And if I'm stepping on your toes right now because you're religious, I'm glad. Because I want to step on your toes!

"But now let me tell you what I *am* passionate about. I'm passionate about getting up and following a God who says, 'Mike, I sent my Son to die for you, and my love for you is unconditional. All you have to do is accept it and share it with the world.'"

That's my passion. And I try to walk it out every day. I just want to love people. At Starbucks, in business, on the phone, in traffic. As simple as it sounds, sometimes it's the hardest thing to do. But loving the people in front of you—now *that's* something I can get excited about.

There are plenty of angry, hurt people in the business world. They're all bound up in past slights and pains and fears, not even free to talk to the person in front of them, let alone love them. Want to know the real reason they're all choked up? Why they can't even really love *themselves*? It's not because of some childhood trauma or daddy issues. It's because their view of God is so screwed up.

When we try to make God like us, we fail. His thoughts are not our thoughts. His ways are not our ways. God doesn't think of me the way I think of me, and He doesn't think of you the way you think of you. God basically says to us, "If you take the time to figure out what I really think of you, then it will change how you look at yourself." And that's what has to change before we can love the people in front of us.

This changes everything—not just the way we see ourselves, but also the way we see and treat other people. It's like falling head over heels in love with someone. The whole world takes on a different color, a different shape. Just like with Jonah!

When I talk about living our passion as businesspeople, that's what I'm talking about. I'm not just sitting around sharing God with people all day long. In my interactions with other human beings, God expresses Himself through me. Walking out your passion in business is the same as walking out your passion in any other area. At the end of the day, it's all about love, because love triumphs over everything.

The moment you let God's love lead you, you're going to reach heights you had never thought possible. I have witnessed firsthand how life-changing this can be. Over the last thirty years, I have worked with thousands of businesspeople and have seen the change in their lives when they let in God's love. And once you change, you bring those changes with you wherever you go. You're no longer living life out of fear of what others think—being a different person depending on where you are or with whom you're speaking. You're not divided.

And when you change who you are, what you do automatically changes. That's the key. Walking out your passion becomes who you are in every aspect of your life.

How are you walking out your passion in the marketplace today?

2

BE YOURSELF IN THE MARKETPLACE

I love to be around people who know why they're alive. Don't you? If we know what we bring to the table and why, then we're living with passion. I've been in the market space for over thirty years, and I've witnessed how passion changes the way we do business. It changes the way we do life.

A lot of people confuse passion with sex. That's not the kind of passion I'm talking about. Passion is adopting God's view of yourself, finding your purpose, and then doing everything you can to live out that purpose.

It's not about being an introvert or an extrovert; you can be completely introverted and have as much passion as an extrovert.

Here's a funny story. I recently called a friend up to offer him a deal. I laid the whole thing out for him.

When I told him the commission he'd be getting, he said, "Holy cow. You've got to be kidding."

About four days later, I was having lunch with him, and I asked, "So what did you think about that deal?"

He said, in a perfect monotone, "It's incredible. I'm so excited about it."

I kept waiting for his demeanor to match his words. Why wasn't he getting excited? This was a huge deal! He should be exclaiming, "This is the most unbelievable deal, Mike! This is great!" That's what I would have done.

Instead, he was sitting calmly, saying, "It is incredible. My wife saw the emotion in me and couldn't believe it. She's excited, too."

And then I realized, it was all in there. It was on the inside of him. He's a different sort of guy than I am; I wear my emotions on my sleeve. But just because he doesn't show it on the outside, does that mean he doesn't have passion in his life? No! Of course not.

I'm going to confess something: sometimes on Saturday mornings, I watch cartoons. Laugh if you want, but I get a lot of inspiration and spiritual insight from them. My favorite is Popeye. Brutus is the bad guy, right? All he wants to do is hurt Olive Oyl, that skinny little thing. He ties her to the tracks and tries to get the train to run over her.

Popeye sees this and does nothing until he gets that can of spinach and squeezes it. He eats it, grows muscles, and saves the day. But do you know what he says before he squeezes the can of spinach?

"That's all I can stands; I can't stands no more."

That's exactly what I think about living a life without passion: "That's all I can stands; I can't stands no more."

I am tired of living a passionless life. I'm tired of being around people who live passionless lives. I want to be around people who know why they're alive and get after it.

Do you know who lived with passion? Teddy Roosevelt. In 1912, he was campaigning for a third term as president, (yes, a third term—the Twenty-Second Amendment was not passed until 1947), giving more than six hundred speeches in one year and traveling twenty thousand miles. When he was in Milwaukee, Wisconsin, he got shot in the chest. And guess how he reacted?

"Don't take me to the hospital," he said. "I'm breathing. I'm OK." He then proceeded to deliver his speech for the next hour and a half and *then* went to the hospital!

What was going on inside Teddy Roosevelt's heart?

That's what I'm after, because if it doesn't happen in my heart, it's all manufactured. Roosevelt may have been a former president, but what mattered more to him was not the title; it was his purpose and passion that inspired him to do what he felt called to do.

Do you know what that is in your own life?

That's what we have to figure out.

I'm passionate about influencing people. I consider myself to be an influential leader. We all have the power to influence somebody, whether it's our employees or coworkers, our kids, or even the Starbucks barista. Passion doesn't take place in the past or in the future; it's *now*. You want to influence someone? Do it. It's not tomorrow; it's today. God put that fire inside you. You just have to uncover it.

When I sit down with someone, I can usually discover his or her passion, whether it's a janitor or a CEO. Unfortunately, the more successful the person, the harder I have to swing a sledgehammer to knock out his or her ego first. You know what ego stands for? E-G-O: Easing God Out. But you don't ease God out of the marketplace He created. You figure out a way to flow with Him in it. That's passion. That's success. And that's what we all want.

But how do you even go about discovering your passion? Many people say that they have no idea what it is. The reality is that everyone is passionate about something. Observe what you say to others. Ask your friends or colleagues what you talk about most.

What would you do if money were not an issue? What do you daydream about most of the time? What is it that makes you smile the most? What are you doing when time seems to fly by? What do you put more energy into than is required (that comes from the heart, not obligation)?

Passion is purpose that is materialized into action with heart, mind, body, and soul.

To put it simply, why are you on this planet?

3

FOR THE LOVE OF BUTTERFLIES

We all have different passions. Some of us love water-skiing. Others are obsessed with reality TV. Maybe you've got a love for hunting, or ladling out soup at a soup kitchen, or baking cookies for your kids.

Your passion could even be a little offbeat, like the guy who's carved out a whole career for himself by playing dead. I'm not kidding; there is a guy who takes photos and videos of himself lying around "dead" in various fabricated accidents—head injury, car crash— then posts them to social media. And it's not like he doesn't have anything else to do; the guy is married with six kids.

If you're lucky, you found a way to turn your passion into a career. You took your love of numbers and became an accountant, or you're a people person who went into human resources. If you're a whiz at copy and clever slogans, maybe you found your way into advertising. Or perhaps you're a salesman who loves to sell. I have a passion for selling also, and I've tried to put it to good use.

Whatever your passion is, I'm cool with it. I'm not here to judge, because if I'm really interested in getting to know you, I'm going to listen to what makes you human, what makes you *you*. It's not only important that I ask what your passion is; it's important that I'm *open* to it. It matters that I really hear you instead of just nodding and blinking and thinking about who won the big game.

If you couldn't guess, I'm the kind of guy who talks to my neighbors on the plane. I figure it's smart to get to know a little about someone before he's snoring on my shoulder.

Last year, I was coming back to Dallas from a business trip to L.A. The guy sitting next to me was a really serious type. He walked on board, opened his laptop, and got right to work before the safety video even started.

I put my hand out and said, "Hi, I'm Mike."

He gave me a nod. Nothing else. So I tried again.

"So, do you live in Dallas or in L.A.? In which city are you doing business?"

"L.A.," he said, without looking up. He just kept typing away. Obviously, the guy didn't want to talk to me. But after about three minutes, I had to give it one more shot.

"So, can I ask you a question?" I said.

"You're going to anyway," he quipped.

"What are you passionate about?"

He closed his laptop and looked at me.

"Are you serious?"

"Dead," I said.

"OK. Butterflies."

Butterflies? Now I'm thinking the guy's pulling my leg because nobody can be passionate about butterflies.

"Are you kidding me?" I asked.

"No. You asked me and I'm being totally honest with you."

"Great! Tell me about butterflies," I said.

And for the next two and a half hours, I learned about butterflies.

Who knew that their wingspan meant something? The thickness of their wings, the way they metamorphose, the size of their cocoon, and even the veins in their wings have meaning. This guy had one of the largest butterfly collections in the United States. All dead, you know, in plastic. But butterflies nonetheless.

Now, I'll be honest: I don't give a flying flip about butterflies. They're pretty, sure, and it's fun to see them land on the plants in my backyard. But if you're looking for someone with a passionate, lifelong interest, I'm definitely not your guy.

Here's the thing: that didn't matter in the slightest. Here's what I said to the butterfly man on the plane:

"You know what? The subject matter you're talking about makes me want to take a nap, but the fact that you're passionate about it is stirring me up on the inside. Because you really *care* about this, man."

He grinned at me.

"You're right; I do. You're the first person I've met who actually seems to care about what I care about. Which is weird, considering I just met you."

Neither one of us slept a wink. When our plane touched down in Dallas, I was fired up, thinking about all the things *I* was passionate about. And this guy was fired up, too. Someone had finally *heard* him, validating the thing he cared about most.

"Thanks, Mike," he said to me, shaking my hand before we deplaned. "Thanks for asking about my passion. Next time I'm jetting off somewhere, I think I'm going to ask the guy sitting next to me the same question you asked me. Because why not?"

Why not, indeed! Give a little, ask a question, and pass it on. The more open we are with one another, the more we open ourselves up to the good stuff: our own passions and interests and loves. And that's the stuff that really counts.

Maybe you work with dozens or even hundreds of other people, and you don't know the first thing about them or what they love. You can change that, starting today. If you've got cubicle mates, take the opportunity to find out what makes them tick. Talk to your boss. Talk to your interns. Talk to your janitor. Once you start opening yourself up to other people's passions, you'll find it opens up a deeper passion in you.

Why is it important to discuss people's passions with them? I think because it takes us to another level. It gets us out of our heads and into our hearts.

Here was this *very* successful businessman discussing butterflies with me. Really? He had *no* idea how I would respond, but he took the chance, and so did I by asking him.

Most of the time we are so self-protective of the little boy or girl inside of us, we can't get close to anyone, let alone share our passion. So the adult steps in and tries to protect the little one from getting hurt yet again.

A friend told me one time that if I wanted people to "bleed" in front of me (emotionally), then I needed to "hemorrhage" first. In other words, be the first one to share a fear, a hurt, a passion. That requires being humble, listening, and not always having the answer.

I remember being at a social event and listening to a first-year attorney out of University of Texas talk about how cool it was to be an attorney, the cases he was working on, how he defeated the district attorney on a few occasions, etc. One of the men listening was a senior partner in one of the most prestigious law firms in the city, a Harvard graduate. This partner listened with humility and genuine interest, making this young man feel good about himself. Not once did he interject who he was or what he did. That is the humility I am speaking about—putting yourself aside and actually feeding into someone else's passion. I learned a ton from that man just through observation.

Not everyone will want to open up in this way, so be the first.

Yes, we are in business to make money. I understand better value, better warranty, better technology, better presentation, better this, and better that. But what about better ways to connect with someone else's passion? Making it about him or her, not you? Relationships and being real trumps the deal!

Would that change your perspective in business?

4

FIND YOUR GIFT

A friend of mine was watching TV recently with his eight-year-old son. They were enjoying a football game, and my friend's son plays football at his elementary school.

My friend paused the game, turned to his little boy, and asked, "Son, do you know why you're a good athlete?"

"Yes, sir, I do," he said.

"Why is that?"

And this eight-year-old said to his father, "Because in my heart, I really enjoy what I'm doing. Football is in my heart, and I love it. That's what makes me a good athlete."

I was floored when I heard that. This isn't a Dallas Cowboys quarterback talking (at least, not yet!). This is an eight-year-old kid. But he gets it. Football is in his heart. He's passionate about it, he desires it, he works at it—and that's what makes him good. It isn't about his talent for the game. It's about his passion for it.

How many of us can say we have that same level of passion inside our hearts for something? *Anything?* It's even rarer to find someone who uses "passion" to describe his or her relationship with God. But isn't that what God wants?

The Creator of the universe doesn't want to be up on some lofty throne, peering down on us like tiny, miserable ants. He wants to be in our hearts, the same way football is in that eight-year-old boy's.

Most people wake up in the morning dreading the day ahead of them. They crawl out of bed, already condemning themselves for something they did or didn't do the day before or for an obsessive thought they know they probably shouldn't be having. *My boss is such a jerk,* they think, or, *I probably should apologize to my wife for that bonehead move, but I won't do it. Not until she apologizes to me first.*

Imagine this:

Every morning, a father meets his little five-year-old daughter at the door of her room and says, "Honey, Daddy hid a gift somewhere in the house for you." She leaves the room and goes to find the gift. This happens day after day after day. How long would it take for that little girl to wake up in the morning with her first thought being, "Daddy has a gift for me!"

I almost never meet people who say to me, "As soon as my feet hit the floor in the morning, Mike, I'm smiling! I'm ready to go! I'm excited I get to face another day because I know it's going to be a blast. I know there are gifts from God for me *this* day."

Even more unusual are the people who wake up saying, "I cannot wait for the day to begin! The people I meet today are in for a surprise, because they're going to walk away from our interactions happier and freer than they were before!"

I don't meet many people like that. But you know what? Those people do exist, because I'm one of them! And I'm not boasting. I'm just telling you how it is. I wake up every day, fired up to share my passion for God with others and to make their day a little bit better. Passion for God doesn't always mean talking about Him, but rather, letting Him love the person right in front of you.

How?

With words and the way you honor them.

Does that mean I don't ever wake up wishing I had done this or that? Of course not! Some days I wish I had a Gulfstream G650 so I could fly anywhere in the world. I'd make people happier all around the globe if I could hop into my jet and fly to Ghana or Saudi Arabia at the drop of a hat. But that's not the life I live. And who cares? It means I get to make people happier at the Starbucks down the street instead.

What's *your* passion? Sports? Cooking? Business? Do you have a passion for the work you do—or the work you wish you could be doing?

It's sad that we don't have more genuine passion in our jobs and careers. Can you imagine what that would be like, if we were all paid to do the work that was truly in our hearts? What a different world it would be!

If you're an entrepreneur, do you have a passion for your product or service? Do you have a passion for HR because you love dealing with other people and making sure everyone is OK? Do you have a passion for health care, serving people who are sick and old? Do you enjoy providing food or clothing or mentorship to those in need?

Another way to ask this question is: *What is in your heart?*

My friend's little boy is good at football because it is in his heart. He doesn't have to force himself to do something he doesn't want to do. He's already got the passion, so the skills and talent have followed in a natural progression. We could all take a cue from that eight-year-old.

Now, I understand that a passion for something doesn't necessarily mean you will be good at it. I am passionate about golf, but as passionate as I am, doesn't mean I will qualify for the Masters; however, that doesn't mean I can't play golf.

What is in *your* heart? Start with God. Because the more passion you have for God, the more space it opens up for other passions. If you let Him, God will light a fire under your feet, guiding you toward the work you should be doing—the work that will make you leap out of bed every morning, ready and excited to start the day. Or He can completely transform how you go about your job right now!

Here's a question for you: What artist sold more albums than anybody in the history of the world?

I ask this question all the time when I speak to audiences. It amuses me how much the answers vary between older and younger audiences. Older groups almost always say, "The Beatles." A younger group might say, "Beyoncé!" or "Jay Z!"

Both are wrong. To the Beatles fans, I say, "No, but good guess. The Beatles are second."

At which point someone inevitably pipes up with, "Michael Jackson!"

"Nope," I say. "He was third. Want a hint?"

The artist who sold the most albums overcame incredible adversity. It was unbelievable what he went through. He knew what he was doing was unique—it was who he was, and he couldn't stop doing it—but he actually flunked music when he took it in school. His teacher said, "You'll never make it."

This guy even auditioned for the Grand Ole Opry, and they sent him away. They told him, "Nobody wants what you've got. You're making a fool out of yourself."

You've guessed it by now, right?

Elvis Presley.

The King.

The whole world told Elvis he'd never make it as a musician. But he believed in himself and never gave up.

We never see the "behind the scenes" reels from other people's lives. We'll never know the demons that haunted Elvis or the complete truth around his death. But if we all believed in ourselves half as much as Elvis did as a young man, it would not only transform the way we do business, it would also transform the way we see ourselves.

He never stopped believing. Aren't those the stories that motivate us the most? Against all odds. Down 0 to 3 in the NBA Finals, and ending up with a 4 to 3 victory. What has to happen inside of us to get that type of determination and drive to never quit, even if we never achieve our dream?

5

A HOME RUN SWING

Can you give me the names of the last ten winners of the Masters Golf Tournament? How about the Best Supporting Actor winner at the Academy Awards for the last ten years?

I love the Academy Awards; they're exciting and glamorous. Same with the Masters. But I'm betting you can't rattle off those ten names for each any more easily than I can. Why can't we?

Because they don't mean anything to us. Not really, not in a long-term, meaningful way. We all think our accomplishments matter so much—the promotions we get, the money we make, our rank among the company salesmen—but at the end of the day, they're just words and titles.

You know who I *can* tell you about? My third grade teacher, Miss Halpern, who sat me in a chair in front of the class and said, "Michael did something that I want to share with everybody." After her story, the whole class stood up and clapped. I'll never forget that because it influenced my life forever.

When I was seven, I had the opportunity to play in Little League in Chicago. I played for the Dodgers, and we were in the World Series of Little League Baseball. When you're a kid, that's huge.

I remember sitting in the dugout in the sixth inning; in Little League, you only play six innings because you'd be there all night if you didn't cut it around that point. So there we were, bottom of the sixth, bases loaded. We're down two runs, and there are two outs. There's so much tension in the air, you could slice it with a knife. My buddy Chucky is up at bat. I look over and he's got his head between his legs.

He looks up at me and says, "I don't feel so good."

"Chucky, what do you mean?" I ask. "You feel fine! You're gonna go up and bat and drive in a run and get this done."

Why did I say that? Because I'm up after Chucky and I don't want to bat. I'm scared to death.

"Nah, man, I don't feel good." And then Chucky starts throwing up all over the dugout. He threw up on the bats and the mitts. He threw up on himself.

The ump comes over and goes, "Hey, Coach. Get your team together. We've got to finish up the game."

So my coach says, "Moore! You're up."

I'm like, "No way. Not me. Chucky, wipe your mouth off and go to bat!" But he can't do it. He's sicker than a dog. So it's up to me.

I'm this tiny little kid. I'm wearing the uniform with the short sleeves, only I'm so small that my sleeves come down past my elbow. I put the helmet on, and it's covering my eyes. The smallest bat is the bongo bat, and that's the one I grab. *Two outs, bottom of the sixth, bases are loaded.* My heart is beating so fast. I'm terrified.

As I walked to the plate, the coach runs over. "Moore! Hold on a second." He gets on his knees, looks me right in the eyes, and says, "Remember this one thing: you've got a home run swing."

"Wow," I'm thinking. "Coach says I have a home run swing!"

So I walked out to the plate, feeling kind of arrogant and cocky, and I look up at the pitcher's mound—and it's like this guy is standing on Mount Everest. He's huge. He's a giant. I'm doing all the things pro players do, or at least I'm trying to: I try to bang my shoes but I miss my shoes and hit my ankle. I'm trying to look like I know what I'm doing, but I have no idea. I'm scared to death.

And then the ump calls out, "Let's play ball!"

I put the bat where it's supposed to be and the pitcher winds up. He throws the ball and I hear the ump yell, "Strike one!"

The pitcher had thrown the ball so fast that I could barely see the thing.

My coach is calling out to me, "Great eye, Mike! I love it! Never swing at the first pitch."

My parents are screaming and shaking the fence. They're worse than the kids! I'm standing there and the ball comes again—and I still don't move.

"Strike two!" calls the ump.

The crowds are yelling like crazy. There's so much commotion in the stands.

"Mike, I love your eye," my coach says to me. "You're looking at the ball. But, Mike, you've got to swing at the next pitch."

I'm thinking, "I can't get the bat off my shoulder, Coach. I can't even see the ball!" I'm scared to death and it's all resting on me.

"You've gotta swing, Mike," says my coach. "You don't have a choice. You've gotta swing."

The pitcher winds up. He throws the ball. I close my eyes. I swing as hard as I can—and I foul tip it. The ball hits the bat and goes into the screen behind me.

I'm feeling confident again. I'm standing there thinking, *I hit the ball! I can do this!* I'm thinking about hitting a home run and a television news helicopter swooping down over the field. They've got cameras, and I'm walking around the bases like a hero while they put a garland on my head. The whole bit—just because I touched the ball.

The crowd is going crazy. The pitcher touches his hat. He throws the ball again. I close my eyes, swing as hard as I can . . . and I strike out.

The other team is jumping up and down. They carry the pitcher off the mound. All the parents are jubilant; they're screaming and yelling. I turn around and look at the dugout. All my friends have their heads down. I start crying. I can't believe that I just lost the game.

I'm dragging my bat back to the dugout when the coach runs up to me. He gets down on his knees. I won't look at him. I'm too ashamed.

"I screwed up, Coach. Chucky should have batted. I wasn't the guy for this."

"Mike, look at me," he says. "Don't ever forget this: You still have a home run swing. Now go out and swing at life, and don't put your bat down."

I remember it like it was yesterday. I stood there thinking, *Who is this guy? Is he God? Is he my dad?*

At the time I wished he were. That man changed my life.

When I get up every morning, there's a God in Heaven saying, "Mike, life is not made up of home runs and grand slams. Life is made up of strikeouts and walks—and maybe sometimes you get a hit, but you have to keep swinging and never put your bat down."

And remember, even the best hitters in the world only hit three out of ten times at bat!

I owe that coach a lot, because he introduced me to a new way of thinking—and a new idea of God. A God that is not looking for deficiencies in my life, but that instead, is reminding me daily of His mercy, compassion, and unconditional love. I'll remember what that coach said for the rest of my life.

I'll tell you who's going to remember you: the people you influence for God. Those are the people who will remember you long after you're gone. Make a billion dollars; I hope you do. Make $50 billion. But you know what? If you're not influencing people for God in the marketplace, if you're not living out your intended purpose, nobody's going to remember you or your money.

What people are going to remember is what you did from your heart for others. If I've learned anything from thirty-plus years in the marketplace, it's that. I've lived all the highs and lows of being a businessman: striving to be number one, being number one, climbing the ladder, pushing people down, hurting people's feelings, saying one thing while doing something totally different, talking about God, not living for God. I've struck out hundreds of times, and I've made some home runs, too. I've done it all. But in the end, all that matters is what we did in our hearts for others.

Ask yourself: What does God want me to do? What's my position on the inside? What is my intended purpose? What am I passionate about? Ask those questions with real humility and the integrity will follow. God's path for you and your life will become clearer.

Part II

GOD'S CURRENCY

6

FAITH AND BUSINESS ARE NOT ANTONYMS

We hear the word "faith" all the time, but almost always in a religious context. Very rarely do we confront the word in a business context; in fact, it feels uncomfortable and strange to do so. We think, *That word doesn't belong in business.*

But you know what? It does.

Faith is simply believing the words of another. It is putting our confidence in something that has been promised. That's all faith is. And if we didn't believe in the words of another, business as we know it wouldn't exist.

I'll give you an example. You may be sitting there thinking, *Well, I don't have a lot of faith.* Sure you do. The sun comes up every day. Do you ever go to bed at night saying, "Honey, the sun may not come up tomorrow. What should we do if that happens?" Not unless you're crazy. The sun comes up every day, and knowing that, you make plans and live your life. That's faith.

It's faith that when I'm driving and a guy stops in front of me, the two lights on the back of his car will light up red. When I see those red lights come on, it means his brakes are on. I believe that when he touches his brakes, the lights are going to come on. I also believe that when I touch my brakes, the lights on the back of my car are going to come on, and somebody's not going to hit me from behind. That's faith.

I believe I'm going to have a job tomorrow morning when I walk into the office. I have faith that I won't come in and find my desk gone and my assistant saying, "You never worked here."

We have faith, and we exercise faith every moment of every day in the business community. We believe what our customers tell us. We believe what our boss says. We believe tomorrow's a holiday, so we don't have to come to work. We believe people, and that's all faith is: believing the words of another.

Let's say I'm flying to Los Angeles on a business trip from Dallas. I have to get on a plane at ten o'clock the next morning. So the night before, I'm all packed and ready to go. And the next morning, as I'm getting ready to leave, I get a phone call from American Airlines.

The lady on the line says, "Sir, we just want to let you know your flight has been canceled. As a matter of fact, all flights are delayed today and your flight will be taking off tomorrow at the same time."

"OK," I say, "thanks for letting me know." What do I do next? I put my bags down, get in my car, drive to my office, and continue doing business in Dallas.

Let's walk through that again. I get a phone call the day I'm supposed to leave. In my mind, I'm traveling from Dallas to Los Angeles to attend a business meeting. I get a phone call from a complete stranger who I don't know. I don't know from where in the United States the phone call has originated, and it's a voice I don't recognize on the other end of the telephone line. I've never met this person and probably never will. She tells me that the plane I'm supposed to be on to fly to Los Angeles for a business meeting in which I'm going to further my career has been canceled. And I go, "Oh, OK," and believe what she says. The proof that I believe what she says is that I take my luggage, put it back in my house, get in my car, and drive to the office. I stay in Dallas, based on the words of a complete stranger whom I have never met.

That is faith.

Now let's redo that and see how it plays out if I don't have faith.

The same woman calls and says, "Hello, Mr. Moore. I just want to let you know that your flight has been canceled. As a matter of fact, all flights to Los Angeles are canceled today and your flight will be taking off tomorrow at the same time."

"Really?" I counter. "I don't know if I believe you. What's your name? Who do you work for? I want to talk to the pilot right now, and then I want to talk to all the flight attendants, because I don't believe you. Maybe you got a call from my competitor and he doesn't want me in L.A. because he knows that if I get to L.A. and close the deal, he won't get the customer. So I don't believe you."

Do we do that? We never do that. Why? Because we believe people. Barring some extreme circumstances, we believe the words of another person.

That's all faith is. So why can't we take the word "faith" that has been stolen by religion and use it on a day-to-day basis? "I believe what you say." "Yeah, I'm full of faith." "I have faith that I'm going to do well in my career." "I have faith that you're going to follow through on what you say."

That's where trust is developed, because the more of what you're saying to me that comes true, the more I believe you. I develop more trust and more trust and more trust. When I've known someone for a year or two, I might trust him or her a little bit, but someone I've known or worked with for ten, fifteen, twenty years? I probably trust him or her a great deal. I believe that what he or she is telling me is true and that my faith is not misplaced.

How much more can we trust in the words of God, the same God who made us? He hasn't just known us for six months or six years. He has known us since before we were born, before we were even conceived. We believe what He says in the Scriptures to Abraham, Isaac, and Jacob, to all the prophets, and to His disciples Paul and Peter and John. And we believe what He says about us. That's faith too.

All of us live in four worlds. We each have a public world, a professional world, a personal world, and a private world.

Our public world is all about image management. We go to the grocery store and see people from a distance, and we think we know them based on some of their behaviors. We go into a coffee shop and make up our minds about everyone standing in line.

In my first book, I talked about the day I saw a guy in line at Starbucks who was absolutely huge. I figured he had to be a weightlifter or a bodybuilder with a pea-sized brain, a third-grade education, and a vocabulary of maybe five words. But I got to know this guy, and he turned out to be a Rhodes scholar. Boy, was I wrong about him! In our public world, we are constantly judging others based on their outward appearance, and they're doing the same thing to us.

Then there's the professional world, and that's the world in which we work. If you're a student, it's your school. If you're a working professional, it's your job. Whether it's a university, a nonprofit, a company, or a corporation, the people in your professional world have a common objective. In school, you're focused on getting an education and passing your classes. In business, you're focused on making a profit and keeping your job. The people you meet in your professional world? You know them on a factual level. You know the basics of their lives: their spouse's name, their kids' names, all that stuff. But you don't know them as well as you know the people in your personal world.

Your personal world is comprised of your best friends and family, including your kids, your parents or spouse. These people know you on an emotional level. They know how you feel, and they know what buttons to push to make you angry. Actually, I shouldn't say "make" you angry. People can't "make" you be anything; you're already what you are. But the people in your personal world know what to say or do to stir up the anger that's already inside you!

And finally, there's your private world. That's the last world, and we live in there alone. No one else is permitted into your private world. No one. It's just you and God. Your purpose comes from your private world; that's where your value is determined. What you believe about God in that area of your life will determine how you walk out your business life.

Most people get it backward. They go out into the first three worlds—public, professional, and personal—to get acceptance and to find their true value. Then they try to bring that back into their private world. But really, it should be working the other way. Your value comes from God. It comes from the relationship you have with Him in your private world. And *that's* the value you bring back into all the other worlds in which you live.

What would it look like if you took that to heart? If you let it change how you interact with people in your family, at your job, and in line at Starbucks? How would your life change if you found your true value in your private world, and then started walking it out in the marketplace every day?

DON'T CHEW MY STEAK

This may seem like a radical statement, what I'm about to say, but I'm going to say it anyway.

First off, let me be clear: I am so grateful for the churches and the synagogues and the temples we have in this world. And I love the programs we have for everybody—ministries for kids and teenagers, Bible studies for women, Bible studies for men, groups for singles and for couples. When I see children singing songs about God, that's beautiful. And when I see people in their seventies and eighties get together to pray and study the Scriptures, I love that.

Here's the problem: businessmen and businesswomen often get overlooked. Many of the people I work with don't feel like there's anything for them at church. They don't hear the truth of God's message. They don't see how it applies to their lives or how to carry it out in the marketplace.

And that's where the modern church really misses the boat. When men and women in the marketplace get a hold of the true Gospel—the forgiveness, mercy, and love of the Lord Jesus Christ—it changes their lives. When the marketplace allows God—the same God who *made* the marketplace—to be a part of it? When we actually look to Him to help us do business the way business should be done? That's when the world will change.

As educated businesspeople, we go to college and we get a degree. Some of us go back to school and get our master's or PhD. We put thousands of dollars and hours into our fields of study, whatever they may be. And then we go to church and listen to our pastor talk about what the Good Book says, which is the book of promises.

Here's my question: Why don't we, as businesspeople, know what it says? We're pretty sharp; we read, we study, we have degrees. Why do we rely on pastors to interpret the Scriptures?

I don't have you chew my food before I eat it, do I? Never in my life have I said, "Hey, can you do me a favor? Here's a steak I just bought at one of the best steakhouses and a $350 bottle of red wine and some vegetables. Can you eat it for me? Just chew it up real nicely. And slosh that wine around your mouth too. Then just spit it all out. Put everything back on the plate so I can eat it." That isn't just disgusting; it's ridiculous.

I'm not the smartest guy on planet Earth, but I can read. I bet you can too. So why are we not reading God's promises for ourselves?

"But, Mike," you say, "I go to church every Sunday and I listen."

Love that. But that's one day a week, man. What about the other six days? Don't you want to know what God's Word says for *you*?

So here's an easy how-to for you:

Step One: Spend five minutes reading something from the Scriptures. It doesn't even matter what; just pick something. Read a passage from God's Word. After you read it, ask yourself: *What is God trying to say to me? What is it that He's trying to speak to me about?*

Step Two: Get a few friends together and have them read the same passage of Scripture. Start a discussion about it. Talk about what that section means to each of you and how it applies to your life. That's when the magic happens. You're having a lively discussion and actually learning something. Instead of getting someone to hand-feed you God's Word, you're chewing into it yourself.

I can go and eat a steak and drink a bottle of wine like any other human being, and so can you. Well, guess what? God's Word is available to every person on the planet! And it's not some mysterious code that you won't be able to understand or interpret. The reason I didn't understand Scripture for so many years is that I never took the time to pick it up, read it, and ask, "Lord, what are you saying to me? What do you have for me as a businessman?"

When you study computer science, you read from a manual. Scripture is just another kind of manual. It's not a to-do list; it's more like a love story. A story that shows how much God wants to have a relationship with you. Don't you want to know how much you're loved?

THE PHOTOGRAPHS IN OUR HEADS

We don't often question what we believe. We don't question our belief system because we live by it. Which is all fine and good if our belief system is right, but what if it's off in some way? And what if the pictures I carry around in my head are very different than the pictures you carry in yours?

This idea is at the crux of everything. When we talk about how to change the marketplace as businessmen and businesswomen, the photographs in our heads are a crucial piece of the puzzle.

A few years ago, I went to a cafeteria in Dallas for lunch. It was the kind of cafeteria in which you sit wherever you want, which means you might sit next to people you don't know. So I'm in line with my food, and I'm talking to the people around me. "Hey, nice to meet you. How are you?" Just getting to know people, because you never know who you'll run into. So I'm talking and enjoying myself, because I love meeting new people.

I get my food and start walking toward a table where a gentleman is already sitting down. He's a good-looking guy with a nice suit on, and he's got a moustache. As I walk closer to the table, I notice the reason he's got a moustache is that he's got a deep scar on his upper lip.

So I sit down and say, "Hey, nice to meet you. I'm Mike. God made an incredible day today, didn't He? It's so beautiful out."

This guy looks at me, takes his tray, gets up, and goes to another table.

And I'm sitting there going, "What just happened? Do I have something on my face? Maybe I'm missing something."

Here's what I was missing: When this guy was a young boy, his dad would always watch the football game on Sunday afternoons. He was a little kid, so of course he wanted to please Dad. So one Sunday, he runs into the kitchen and goes, "Mom, I want to bring Daddy his favorite food and beer so he can watch the big game!"

Mom thinks this is really sweet. She fixes a sandwich and pours a cold beer into a nice, tall glass and puts everything on a tray. Just picture in your mind this little boy who loves his dad. He's going to take care of his dad, and he's excited. He's holding this little tray, and he walks out to surprise his father. He tiptoes into the room and Dad's watching the game. And as he gets close to his dad, he trips and the tray flies out of his hand onto the glass coffee table in front of his father. It shatters everything. There's beer all over the place, and shards of glass.

His dad is interrupted, obviously. He's so upset that he takes his hand and swings it, hitting his little boy in the face. He happens to have a college ring on and it hits his son in the lip, and the boy starts bleeding. They bring him into the kitchen, and his dad's yelling at him, "What did you do that for?! I can't believe you were that stupid!" Meanwhile, the kid is bleeding and his mom is saying to his father, "Honey, I can't believe you did this." And suddenly, there's a big argument going on.

In the middle of all this, while they're holding a towel to the boy's lip to keep it from bleeding, the phone rings. The dad picks up the receiver.

"Oh, Pastor, hi," he says. "No, no, no, no. You are not bothering us, Pastor, not at all. As a matter of fact, we were just having a little Bible study with the family, discussing God and things like that. What can I do for you?"

"You are a faithful guy," the pastor says. "We need you at church tonight."

"Pastor, you know you can count on this family. We'll be there. We'll have our children with us. You know you can count on us because we love the Lord, Pastor."

He continues, "Hey, Pastor, God bless your day." And he hangs up.

What does his son think?

Why does my father hate me? Why does God hate me?

And here it is, thirty-some-odd years later. I walk into a place of business to get food and I sit down with a man I've never met before and I say some simple words: "God made an incredible day today, didn't He? It's so beautiful out." And what does he hear? "God hates me." So he gets up, thinking, *That man reminds me of my father. I don't want to be around him.* And he goes to another table to get away from me.

I didn't know all of this then, of course, but I know it now from spending more time with this man. The point is: I don't know the view of God you have. I don't know how you were raised. I don't know what you're thinking. I don't know if when you look up, you see a disciplinarian. Do you see a cosmic killjoy? Do you see a God who's standing in Heaven with a book of notes criticizing you? Or do you see a God who says, "Come to me, I want to show you who I really am—a God of unconditional love, mercy, and grace."

What does that mean for us, as men and women in the marketplace? We have to dare to believe the goodness of God. We have to believe that He will wipe away the scars and heal our true selves beneath them. Isn't that why he sent his Son to us in the first place?

We might spend the better part of a lifetime trying to stay hard and calloused, but all the while, God is right there, ready and willing to take away all our mistakes, all the things we've done wrong, all the wrong that has been done *to* us, and all the sin—past, present, and future.

If that's true, if He does do that, then we have to dare to change our system of belief, which will change our feelings. God is not out to get us.

Is the world going to agree with us? No. You think it's easy in business to walk this out? No! But here's what I do know. To be as settled as I am in my private space, in my private world, to know the love of God, to know the mercy of God, to trust completely that He has got my back—knowing all that allows me the freedom to give to other people without expecting something in return.

The guy with the scar on his lip? He and I were talking about two different gods. The God he saw and the God I was talking about were two completely different pictures in our brains. I have a certain "photo" in my brain when I talk about God. And this man had his own photo. We think people know the photo *we* see on the inside, but it's hardly ever the same photo that *they* have captured on the inside.

So what do we do about that? Is it the listener's responsibility to ask, "Can you tell me what you mean by that? Or can I be more articulate with the words I'm communicating so you can see the photograph on the inside of my head?"

I certainly know what it's like to carry around baggage from childhood, especially to feel like you grew up with a dad who didn't appreciate you. I was born and raised in Chicago. We would get some awful weather in February; the snow was crazy. I remember that 1979 contained one of the craziest snowfalls to ever hit Chicago. My dad had to go to work. We didn't have a garage because he wanted us to have a bigger backyard to play in. So there was no garage for the cars, which meant that when there was a blizzard, he would go outside and the car would be encased in snow.

I remember that I got up that morning and thought, *I'm going to please Dad.* I went out and got the broom and the shovel, and I spent an hour uncovering his snow-covered car. I got out there and cleaned up everything. I shoveled all the walks and made everything perfect.

So my dad stepped outside and I was standing there, waiting. Waiting for him to say "Thanks," waiting for his amazement, waiting for something. And he just got in his car and drove away.

I was so mad. I kept thinking, *I did all this. You can't acknowledge me?* And I remember hearing this voice inside of me, asking, *Did you do it for the acknowledgment, or because you wanted to do it?*

For God, it's always the latter. He does it because of who He is, not because of what we do. That is the foundation we need to understand. God moves because of Himself, not because He needs something from us. To believe that, to have it truly change our heart, to have that change take hold—that's going to change the way we deal with other people. We will see Him differently, so differently than the man I met at the cafeteria with the scar on his lip.

I did get to know that man. I invited him to a couple of events at my house, and he came. The fact that I got close enough to him that he would visit my home was pretty amazing. I haven't seen him in years, but meeting him was a really important lesson for me, a reminder that we all walk around with photographs in our heads, and they're each unique to us.

As businesspeople, given the variety of people we get to work with, we have an incredible opportunity to spend time discovering the photographs of God in other people's heads, and then share our own full-color, high-resolution version of God with them.

In this next week, with whom will you share your amazing photos?

9

"NO, LORD, KEEP 'EM"

Every month I have people over to my house for "not your average" meeting. I try to facilitate an environment where businessmen and businesswomen can come together and speak honestly about what they're struggling with and the lessons they're learning. Then I bring in speakers who share their real-life experience of how God has changed their lives. Not the God of behavior modification, but the God of the universe who took away our sins.

As we all know, it can be difficult to meet new people and become exposed to new ideas. We go to our job and eat at the same restaurants and get coffee at the same Starbucks and shop at the same grocery store and then go home to the same family (hopefully!) every night. So where are you going to meet people? I figure, if people can hear about God in a safe environment that's not a church and, in the process, meet like-minded men and women they never would have met in the market-place—great! I've done my job. I like to think of my house as a place for people to come and network and get to know each other.

One of the speakers we've had who really made an impression was Nick Vujicic, a man born in Australia with a very rare congenital disorder. Nick has no arms and no legs. His story is pretty remarkable; Google him, and you'll see why. As an evangelist and motivational speaker, Nick travels the world, sharing his message and inspiring millions of people. He even started his own nonprofit, Life Without Limbs.

The night Nick spoke, hundreds of people came to listen to him. He's the messenger of hope. This guy had a better attitude than any of the people in that room who had both of their arms and legs!

Nick's overarching message was, "It's all about what God did for me." Not what God took from him or didn't do for him.

After he spoke that night, Nick stayed over at my house. Once everybody else had gone home, he and I got to talking.

At one point I asked, "Nick, have you ever wondered why you don't have arms and legs? Do you ever want them?"

"Mike," he replied, "I tried to kill myself so many times. There was a time when I prayed and said, 'God, I want you to grow arms and legs for me.'"

Nick truly believed he was going to wake up one day with arms and legs, because he was praying to the God of the universe.

But one day, not long after he'd made this prayer request, he felt like God was asking him a question: "Hey, Nick, if I give you your arms and legs, but then ten, or twenty, or fifty million people around the world don't hear your message of hope, and then don't invite me into their hearts to change their lives, do you still want your arms and legs?"

And Nick said, "No, Lord, keep 'em."

Wow! That blew my mind. Only a God of mercy and grace can change a heart like that. You could line up every self-help specialist or life coach in the world and you won't get that kind of transformation.

Think about all the martyrs we've read about in the Bible—and there are plenty to choose from. Do you think the apostles Paul, Peter, John, James, Matthew, and Luke all died for a God who was strictly interested in behavior modification? No one's dying for a God like that.

I'll tell you who you would die for: a God who says, "You've done nothing to prove to me that you're going to walk out the gift that I gave you, but I'm all in. I've taken away all your sin—past, present, and future. Now go walk that out. You're free."

That's a message you can die for. And that's a message that will change every aspect of your life—at work, at home, and beyond.

Believe it or not, most people in the marketplace are waiting to talk about this. Are you ready for the conversation?

10

THE REAL SUPERMAN

A few years ago, the CEO of a Texas company was featured in a well-known magazine. It was a great piece about how he was not only the top CEO of a well-respected corporation, but how he was also a family guy. This man seemed to have it all; he'd earned a lot of money for himself through stock options and had made a lot of money for his shareholders, but he'd also maintained a great marriage. Despite all his other responsibilities, he still made time to coach his kid's soccer team. He was on the school board and involved in various community-service projects.

I remember reading this article and thinking, *Wow, what a résumé! What an upstanding guy.* It's rare to encounter somebody at that level in a corporation who also has time to coach a soccer team and be that

involved in the community. But this guy did everything. He was like Superman. *What an incredible life!*

Or so I'd thought.

Over time, I had the opportunity to do business with his company, and I got to know this gentleman. I loved walking into restaurants with him because everybody knew this guy. It was kind of like walking into a restaurant with the pope or the president. Suddenly, everybody is clamoring to get to know you because of who you know.

So we started having lunch together, and before long, I got to know this guy personally. He really opened up to me.

"Mike," he said one afternoon, "I'm not sure you know this, but you know my wife?"

I replied, "Yeah, sure." By then I'd met his wife a few times.

"She's not my first wife," he said. "She's my fourth."

"Whoa," I said. I'd truly had no idea. "I thought you guys had gotten married when you were teenagers, and you'd been together forever!"

He shook his head.

"As a matter of fact, our marriage isn't doing too well."

"I'm sorry to hear that," I said, even more surprised than before. Remember, on the outside, this guy had everything.

"I've just broken off an affair I was having," he said. "My wife didn't know about it, but it doesn't matter. It's over now."

Now this was after about three martinis, so this guy was really opening up.

"Let me share something else with you, Mike," he said. "I've been in and out of AA for over twenty years."

I looked down at the martini he was holding and back up at him. The whole thing was unbelievable. In my mind I flashed back to that newspaper article I'd read, the one that had painted this gentleman as a larger-than-life leader. And now here he was, sharing his personal struggles with me.

"You know, Mike," he said, leaning in. "I'm not a homosexual, but once I had a homosexual experience just for the thrill of it." His expression darkened. "Recently, I've had some really deep thoughts about suicide."

My jaw dropped. I was seeing two totally different sides of who I thought this person was. The résumé, the myriad of accomplishments, the achievements—those all belonged to one side. But here I was, getting to know him heart-to-heart as he shared all of his personal struggles. A little voice inside me said, *Mike, how do you want to know this man? Do you want to know him based on his of achievements, his performance, his accolades, and his exterior? Or do you want to know him based on the struggles and failures in life that he's facing? Because, Mike, that's how you look at people. You define a person by his exterior and by what he's done, either by how good (how impressive his achievements) or how bad (how much he's failed). Then you decide how you're going to view that person based on one or the other.*

I knew then that God was speaking to me. He was teaching me an important lesson about judging people *not* by their external identity, but by their true identity at heart.

We can all judge our coworkers, friends, and family members either by how successful they are (the good), or how much they've screwed up (the bad). But there is a third way to know somebody, and that's the way the Creator of the universe views people. It's totally different than the way we do it—and infinitely better.

God isn't looking at our résumé. He's not looking at our failures, and He's not looking at our "greatest hits" list, either. No matter how you define yourself—as a businessman, a spouse, a parent, a neighbor—your true identity lies in Christ. If you want to become what you were created to be, then you must turn to Jesus Christ for the forgiveness of your sins. That is true success! That will set you up for real living.

That day at lunch, I prayed that God would help me start looking at people differently. We can compare ourselves and measure our lives against each other forever—and we're going to feel we're better than some people and worse than others. To this day, I can't believe I actually had the audacity to sit there thinking, *This guy's been divorced three times. At least I've only been divorced once.*

But you know what? The ground is level where Jesus Christ died on a cross for our sins. Rich, poor, divorced, married, black, white, female, male, young, old—it doesn't matter. The billionaires in the 1 percent are exactly the same as the woman who has $200 in her checking account. For any and all of us, Jesus Christ is the only way to obtain forgiveness of our sins, and that gift is 100 percent free.

Do you realize that the greatest need of the human heart is to know it is forgiven?

11

AN AUDIENCE OF ONE

I have no competition because I'm not competing with anybody.

What if that were your motto for doing business? Better yet, what if it were your motto for doing *life?*

This saying is one of my greatest guideposts. If I think about all the people I'm competing with—in sales, in speaking, in publishing—I will drive myself crazy. Instead, I get up and do my best every day, and I don't have to think about what the other guy is doing, because there *is* no other guy. Life isn't a competition.

Here's another great motto for you to contemplate: *My audience is one.*

It's a play on words because you can spell it two ways: O-N-E or W-O-N. *My audience is won.* And, for our purposes, both statements are true.

Here's what I mean. Let's say I'm a stage actor, one of the greatest in the world. I walk out onto the stage to perform, and there's only one person in the audience: God.

But God's not sitting there with a basket of tomatoes, ready to pelt me if I miss a line.

He says, "I love watching you. Even though I'm the one who made you, I love sitting in the front row and watching you perform."

"But I've done it a million times, God."

"And every time you do it, it's fresh for me. Encore! Encore!"

That's God. He's our audience of one, and He's not judging. He's already completely won over before we say a single line.

Compare that to the rest of the world, the people who are ready to pelt us with tomatoes at a moment's notice. Our souls ask for bread, and we're fed stones. We all want to be loved and cherished, but we end up feeding ourselves stones when we go elsewhere for unconditional love and acceptance. We numb ourselves with too many drugs or too much alcohol or pornography, or we become workaholics, desperately seeking that applause. We're always playing to an audience, somewhere, and they're always ready to devalue us. They might not even mean to—they just don't have the power to give us value one way or another.

Why not accept our audience of one, the God of the universe! He wants so much to cheer us on and give us his thunderous applause. We don't need to keep dancing desperately for love and approval; there is no competition. We might as well stop fighting a battle that has already been won/one!

What weapon do you fight with?

Is it time to put it down?

12

DEAD RABBITS OR LIVE TURTLES

When was the last time you got hung up on something you didn't have? Maybe it was a person—that guy in the next cubicle you're just *dying* to go on a date with—or a thing, like a big promotion at work. Maybe it was the shiny new car you saw in the parking lot, or that fabulous designer outfit on display at the mall. Whatever it was—person, job, car, couture—you got it stuck in your head that you absolutely *had to have this thing* to be happy. And if you didn't get it? Fuhgeddaboudit.

What if I told you that something just as good, if not better, was coming down the pike, but you're so miserable and focused on what you *don't* have that you can't even see it?

A few years ago, I met a woman at a coffee shop, and because I like talking to people, we started talking about her life. She told me a story about something that had recently happened to her and her son. Every week, a student in his kindergarten class had the opportunity to bring in something for show-and-tell. Her son had been planning to take his two-year-old white rabbit into school. He had his speech all prepared. He was going to say, "This is a rabbit. This is why it wiggles its nose, and this is why it eats leafy green vegetables." He was very excited.

On the morning of show-and-tell, he got up early and ran into her bedroom, sobbing. At the top of his lungs he screamed, "Mom! Mom! The rabbit died!"

She got out of bed and saw that, sure enough, the rabbit had died during the night. It was lying belly up in its hutch, its black eyes wide open.

"Honey, you just go get ready for school," she told him. "Go take a shower and don't worry."

She then went into the kitchen and said a little prayer.

"Lord," she prayed, "my son wanted this so much. I mean, what can I do?" She admitted that, deep down, she was praying for a miracle. If God could just bring that rabbit back to life—if He could resurrect that animal like He resurrected his own beloved Son—things would be OK.

Still, she knew that was a lot to ask. Maybe it would be better if God could provide *another* rabbit, a stand-in rabbit for the one that had died. She frantically ran through a list of all their family and friends, trying to think if anyone else had a rabbit her son could "borrow" for the day.

But nobody had a rabbit. Was there a way she could make the rabbit *look* alive? Could she prop it up in a shoebox, and from far away it would look mostly normal, and maybe they could pass it around the class very quickly and the other kids could pet it and feel how soft it was but not look at it long enough to know it was dead?

The woman shook her head, shocked at her own obsessive, morbid thoughts.

She opened the door to the garage and there, smack dab in the middle of her welcome mat, was a pond turtle. Her heart soared.

She presented the turtle to her son.

"Look, honey!" she exclaimed. "We've got a turtle! This is what happens when he gets scared: he puts his head inside his shell. He swims around in water and these are his feet."

She couldn't believe what fortune she'd had to find this turtle in the nick of time. And her son couldn't have been more excited. He took the turtle to show-and-tell and the other kids loved him.

Here's what I said to her: "Wow! That's an amazing story! How far was the pond from your house?"

She shrugged.

"Maybe a mile away," she said.

"A mile away," I said. "You have a turtle sitting on your doorstep and the pond is a mile away. When did God set the turtle in motion to get to your house, and how did the turtle know what house to choose, and how did it know to show up on your mat at the exact time you needed it? How did he get into the garage?!"

"Wow!" she exclaimed. "I've never thought of it like that. God must have set the turtle in motion . . . gosh, four days ago, at least. When the rabbit was still alive!"

We had a great discussion about it, and it made me realize something. In life, we're always trying to resurrect dead rabbits, while God is busy sending us turtles. And we need to look around and see the turtles that God is sending, instead of looking at the dead rabbits we think are going to bring us happiness.

Sometimes we think only one thing can make us happy. Meanwhile, there are turtles all around us. We get fixated on dating *that* person or winning *that* job or buying *those* jeans, and meanwhile, there's a bounty of other people, jobs, and jeans that might be even *better* for us. We need to train ourselves to look around and think, *Wait a minute. Maybe there's something better than what I think is best for me.*

For us to get there, we have to be willing to loosen control. Now I have heard people my whole entire life tell me that we need to "Let go and let God." It's a nice idea, but it doesn't work that easily. There is a difference between letting go of control and loosening control. No one ever gives up total control. It's impossible. Think of all the ways you control your life today. Make a list. You manage your diet, exercise, your bedtime, when you wake up, where you work, who you marry, where you vacation; the list is endless.

But look at the things we never control. Make a list. The weather, when you are born, the color of your skin, your height, the past, the next president of Armenia (unless you live there, in which case you can make a difference), the heat of the sun—the list is endless.

I submit that choosing to loosen control will reveal opportunities and magnify "turtles" around you that you may not have seen before.

Are you open to that possibility?

What would that mean in your place of business?

How would this perspective change the way you do business?

13

BE LIKE A GRAPE

How often in life do feel like you're being pressed from all sides? Most of us feel like that pretty regularly. Our rent is due. Our dog is hungry. Our spouse or our kids or our siblings have certain expectations of us that are impossible for us to live up to. We've got that deadline at work and those forms that need to be filed and that presentation to give, not to mention the pressure we're feeling from the big changes we know we need to make in our lives—eliminating old habits that don't serve us and belief systems that are no longer true.

Do you ever wonder how you're possibly going to survive all this pressure and come out all right on the other side?

Not too long ago, I was at Oktoberfest, a yearly beer festival in Germany, and we were all in the big tent, drinking and eating and talking about wine when I had an epiphany.

I said, "Do you realize that wine is the new golf?"

My friends looked at me as if I were nuts.

"What do you mean, 'wine's the new golf'?"

"Think about it," I said. "I take a few clients golfing. It takes us about an hour to get to the course, get dressed, and warm up. It's a four-hour round, minimum. Then when we're done, we go into the clubhouse, have a beer, and talk about who lied the most on the course. Suddenly, six hours have passed, and we get in our cars and go home. All in all, it's a seven-hour event for four guys to get together and bond."

I leaned forward.

"The problem is, our wives aren't there. So wine is the new golf. Because when we go to a wine club, we can still enjoy a long, leisurely day—but this time, we can bring our wives along. We can sit down and talk about the different grapes, and think to ourselves, *Wow, this tastes great!* Now our wives are involved in the conversation, and we guys feel different because we've got them around us. We're still ourselves, but we're being more real."

Everyone agreed that men are significantly more real and tender when they're with the women in their lives.

"Now let's take a step back," I said, "and look at how wine applies to life."

"It takes three years for grapes to grow, right? And they grow in different soils in different countries. So you've got the Sangiovese grape that grows in Italy, the Tempranillo grape that grows in Spain, and the Cabernet and Merlot grapes that grow in France. Some soils are limestone; some are gravel. Some are on slopes facing the sun; some are on slopes facing away from the sun. Some grow on flat land; some grow in mountainous regions. Some are near the sea, and some are in the middle of the country. So you've got different climates and countless varieties of grapes—kind of like human beings."

The thing is, we're all different. Some people grow up in the United States; others grow up in France, Italy, the United Kingdom, Australia, China, or any of the 196 countries in the world. As people grow up in different kinds of soil, in very diverse cultures and belief systems, they grow into different kinds of people. Much like grapes, people develop different vines, different roots, and different fruit.

And what happens with grapes? You take them, you squeeze them, and you create juice. When you go to the store and buy Welch's grape juice, you're essentially buying squeezed grapes.

But here's what's cool. When you want to make wine, you take some of the finest grapes, crush them, and then leave the skins in the juice for a set period of time. How long you leave them there is up to the wine-maker. Once he or she decides the skins have been in there long enough, they are moved to special tanks where they sit for six to twelve weeks. That's how a winemaker matures the grapes.

From there, they may put them into oak barrels— American oak, French oak, Slovenian oak, you name it—where they sit anywhere from a few months to many years, depending on what kind of wine you want (that's up to the winemaker, too). The longer it ages, the better the wine, especially for an Italian or French vari-etal. Now we're speaking mostly of red grapes. There are some whites that age, but I digress.

So I'm sitting there, explaining this to my friends at Oktoberfest, and I start to draw the connection between wine and human beings.

"When we get pressed," I asked, "what do we want to do? We want to run!"

When life's difficulties come our way, they're pressing us hard. We're getting squashed and squeezed, and we don't like it. You think the grapes like to get squeezed? No! They love being on the vine. "Please," they say. "Just let me stay on the vine forever! It's so comfort-able here."

But until the grapes are pulled away from the vine and crushed—until they die—they are incapable of ever becoming wine, the same stuff that we sit there drinking while exclaiming, "No way this wine can taste this good!" The grapes are destined to forever be small and inconsequential, doomed to a fate of either being shriveled by the hot sun or ingested by wild animals or birds.

Isn't it the same way with our lives?

My friends around the table had all grown up in different countries. They represented many different varieties of people, grown on many different kinds of soil. But we all agreed that we get pressed by life, in one way or another. Divorce, bankruptcy, death in the family, disappointment, heartbreak, scandal, unemployment, lost friends, career letdowns, disability, illness, negativity, failure to "live up to our potential," pride, lust, jealousy, crises of faith. Sometimes these things crush us—but they don't have to. Not if we allow ourselves to be shaped into something better.

If we allow the pressing to do what it's supposed to do in our life, we will be turned into something so much better than we were before. The winemaker (God!) will make sure we are pressed properly, so that the pressing does what it's supposed to do, and so that He can produce a wine that makes the world say, "I want that. That's good stuff!"

Sometimes the pressures we face do not feel right. We might be pressed to change our belief system, something we've been clinging to for decades, perhaps even knowing it is flawed. But if your beliefs are hurting you, then your belief system needs to be challenged, and you need to start challenging the way you think.

Imagine a stream of water that's been coursing down a mountain for one thousand years. It's going to travel down that same groove that it first cut into the rock a thousand years ago. How do you change its direction, send it down a different groove? You build a dam.

You tell yourself, "I'm not going to believe this anymore."

And you start believing a different way.

It might take one year or a lifetime; however long it takes, you will eventually be able to form another groove in your mind. Stay open to God and He will change you into something spectacular, just like that amazing bottle of wine.

Bruce Lee said, "Be like water."

I say be like a grape.

Part III

MARKETPLACE
RELATIONSHIPS

♥ | 💰

14

RELATIONSHIPS: THE SMALL PRINT

Anybody can do a transaction. Anybody can do a deal. But not nearly as many people can maintain a relationship.

When you maintain a relationship with a client, there are three unspoken things that transpire. These things relate to the relationship side of business; they're often the things that, in my own experience, transform a client into a friend. Most of us don't take the time to articulate them, but let's give it a shot.

1. Listening

In a relationship, becoming a better listener than a speaker is the first point in connecting. If I am truly listening to what you're saying, I'm allowing you to influence me with the words you're speaking because I'm giving credence to what you're saying. I am actually hearing it and thinking, *Great! How does this apply to my life? How is what you're saying to me changing the way we are relating to each other?*

2. Asking Questions

If I'm focused on building a meaningful business relationship, I'm asking you questions for two reasons. The first is that I need more information. The second is that I need to better understand what I think you're telling me to make sure I am listening fully and listening well.

When this is happening in both directions—when both parties are adapting and listening to one another—something occurs that's beyond a transaction. The transaction will occur based on what we've developed on the relationship side.

3. Spending Time

I need to spend time with you outside of a business setting to demonstrate that I've listened. This is how I prove to you that the questions I've asked, I have internalized, and then we can walk that out together.

Now, I understand I have to make money as a businessman, which means I have to get into business relationships in which I am producing results. But that takes care of itself when a real relationship is present.

I am going to do whatever I can to make sure it's a win-win, not a win-lose. I'm committed to that. I know that I may not "win," but that's not going to affect the relationship. The question is: If I never win, does the relationship go away? Is the relationship based on me getting something? Or is this a true relationship, one that will persevere through both the highs and the lows?

Listening, asking questions, and spending time. That's how to build and maintain a relationship in three easy steps. When these things are in place, trust and loyalty are the natural byproducts. Loyalty is simply showing your clients and colleagues over time that you're there, you're listening, you're asking questions, and you're spending time with them.

Now, of course, there will be times when you meet resistance in any relationship, business or personal. Resistance is great! I love to exercise, and I've learned how to use those thick rubber bands to add resistance to a workout. The more you face resistance, the more your muscles grow.

That's the sort of resistance God offers us. He created all things. He made the universe. God is basically saying, "Here are all my promises to you. But in this world, you're going to meet resistance."

God has given you everything you need in His book of promises to live this life, but He's also going to put some resistance out there for you.

It's like the concepts of good and evil. People say, "I can't believe there's evil." Well, you wouldn't understand good without evil, right? You wouldn't understand "down" if you didn't understand "up." Without those opposites that form resistance in our lives, how would we ever grow?

And where does that resistance play itself out the most? In relationships. Because you can't be in a close relationship with anybody, whether it's your spouse or a business associate, without getting into conflict along the way. There are just going to be times when that transaction will end up being the resistance, and you'll work through it. You will get to the other side and you'll keep working.

Once we get these concepts—listening, asking questions, and spending time—it will change the way we do business. How would the marketplace change if this first changed us?

15

MAKE THE CONNECTION

Are you one of those people who can talk to anyone from anywhere about anything? Or do you have
a hard time finding a point of connection with those
who are different from you? Do you feel closed off
and disconnected from other human beings, maybe
even a little suspicious of their intent?

So much of business is built on trust, and it's impossible to establish trust between people without a basic
point of connection. Every good business relationship is built on authentic connection between human
beings, and if you can't find the places of intersection
and common ground, you cannot truly connect.

I was recently in London as a part of my sommelier
(wine expert) training. One night I was out on the town
with some of the other trainees, having dinner at this
really cool restaurant up in the OXO Tower overlooking

the River Thames. These guys all know a great deal about food and wine, so it was easy enough to engage in conversation. We had a point of reference, a predetermined way of relating to one another.

Then our server came over to check on us. He had a thick accent and wavy black hair. He was obviously not a native Brit.

"Are you enjoying your meal tonight?" he asked.

"We're having a wonderful night," I said. And then, because I was genuinely interested, I asked, "Where are you from?"

"I'm from Macedonia, sir."

"Wow! I love your country!" I exclaimed. I told him how I'd spoken in the spring to a group in Macedonia, what local foods I'd liked best, and even which hotel I'd stayed in.

He looked at me, surprised and impressed.

"No one knows about my country," he said.

"The Greeks don't like that you stole the name Macedonia, right?"

"Exactly!" he said, laughing.

After our server had gone back to the kitchen, one of the other guys in my party turned to me and asked, "Mike, how do you engage with people the way you do? Especially when they're from such a different background?"

I shrugged.

"It's just finding a point of connection. That's the beginning point of any relationship: finding something we have in common and then going from there."

I may be an intense guy, but if you're a total stranger, I'm not going to run up to you and say, "Hi, I'm Mike. Tell me how you feel." You're not going to appreciate that! What if I had challenged this guy from Macedonia on his politics? I could have said, "Do you like our president? Tell me what you think of our leader." That's not a way to build a relationship. In fact, it's a good way to end one before it begins (assuming this person doesn't like our president).

The key is to find something outside of us, a point of connection about which both people can get excited. That's the most authentic way to engage another person, and it holds true in business, with close friends, in social interactions—pretty much all relationships. Which explains why, as the guys and I walked down the Thames after our meal, I felt connected to everybody—kids on skateboards, women jogging, men talking on their cell phones.

We have far more that connects us than drives us apart. God made each of us in His image, which means there's going to be an infinite number of possible connection points.

Look for the stuff that fires people up. Look for the topics that make them speak a little more quickly or passionately. Listen to what people say; this will give you insight into interests or opinions you may share.

If you can carry this attitude into the workplace, it can take a business relationship that was formerly adversarial and turn it into a positive partnership. It can transform a foe into a friend, a competitor into a colleague.

Do you believe this kind of radical thinking can completely change your world? If so, what's your next step?

16

THE COLD CALL

If you're in business, you've probably found yourself wondering how to walk the line between your faith and your job. Is it OK to talk to your colleagues about God? Is it appropriate to share the Gospel with others in the workplace? When should you talk about your faith, and when should you button up?

To answer that, I want to tell you a story.

In 2000, I was getting ready to change jobs. As part of the deal I'd cut with the new company, they had agreed to throw a new car into the mix. I found a dealership out in California that had one I liked. It was a white Mercedes, and it hadn't been titled. So I called this place up, and I got a salesman named Fari.

Fari and I went back and forth over the phone for three weeks, trying to cut this deal. We were negotiating like crazy. The car was a 1999 and the 2000s were already on the market. It was white with gray interior. I'd bought enough cars to know that 99 percent of men want a black car, not a white one. So I knew I had an advantage.

And then, in the middle of all this, as we were negotiating, bargaining, and working through the logistics, I started talking to Fari about my relationship with God.

"I'm pretty extroverted," I told him, "but I'm not religious. I hate religion. Religion is so often tripped up by rules and regulations and man figuring out how to reach God. God has already reached man; that's the relationship."

Fari was completely blown away by this concept. As a Muslim, he had never thought of God as someone he could have a personal relationship with.

The more Fari and I talked, the more I felt a strong need to help him understand that there was a God in Heaven who loved him and wanted to give him the free gift of eternal life.

As it turned out, Fari's mom was a Christian who had converted from Islam. She talked to Fari about God's love, too, but he didn't listen. She was an older woman, and she sat around playing chess and talking about things that happened fifty years ago. Whenever she spoke to her son about God, he shut her out.

But here I was, on the same level as this guy. We were both businessmen, trying to cut a deal. I wanted him to realize that there were businessmen in the world carrying a flag around that wasn't all about sales and profits; my flag was the mercy and goodness of God. So I shared God's mercy and goodness with him over the phone. I told him to do his own research if he wanted.

"You don't have to believe me," I said. "Just listen to the logic I'm using. If it's logical, and if it's God, wouldn't you want to know Him?"

Three weeks later, Fari Saba and I cemented the deal. I traded in my car, even though he'd never seen it; I shipped it to Newport Beach from Dallas sight unseen.

The head of the dealership in California said to Fari, "Are you crazy? What are you doing? We don't know this guy from Adam!"

"My name is on the line," Fari said. "I trust this guy completely."

And then Fari came to Dallas to pay me a visit.

Fari stayed at my house for two days. I took him to a basketball game, took him out to eat, and took him to a car dealership in Dallas to inquire about a potential job. We became friends. I found out he was divorced with three kids. I went out to California and met his mother. The three of us sat down together, and Fari decided to believe that God was in control of his life.

Fast-forward to the present. A few days ago, I got a call from Fari. He had just attended a sales luncheon in Newport Beach, at which he was the speaker.

"I told them about you, Mike," he said. "I told them how you changed my life. I said, 'Let me tell you how to do business.' And then I spent half an hour talking about how we met over the phone. I told our story in excruciating detail. People were crying by the end!" He laughed. "They came up to me afterward and said, 'Your story is amazing, Fari.' And I told them, 'That's the way business should be done.'"

Fifteen years ago, my motive started out as a pretty simple one: I wanted to get a car. But the relationship side of business is everything. Along the way, I made a friend. I even had the opportunity to meet his mom.

Today, Fari is walking with God. He's a different man. All this came about because we'd crossed paths in making a business deal. Sure, I had to get a car, and he had to make a sale. That happened. But there was something deeper. That's what I mean when I talk about the relationship side of business. And that's what I'm after when I'm doing business with people.

Today, many years later, Fari Saba is standing up in front of hundreds of salespeople saying, "Let me tell you how to do business."

The next time you find yourself wondering whether to share your faith or keep quiet, think about Fari. Think about his amazing story, and how the more you focus on the relationship side of business, the more you'll get to be part of amazing stories yourself.

Who's the Fari in your life?

17

SUCCESS IN SELF-DISCLOSURE

Every Wednesday morning, I host an event called "Man Morning." I facilitate the group, and anywhere from thirty to forty men show up and share what they're learning and what God is telling them in their own life.

There's no right or wrong. The key to Man Morning is that we don't sit around judging each other. We simply allow God to express Himself through the various personalities we have in the group. There are extroverts and introverts, feelers and thinkers, and God expresses Himself differently through different people.

Man Morning is a venue for men to get together and be honest and open and real, to sort of "test out" that honesty and openness around other men before bringing it into the marketplace.

We're all professionals and business leaders. We influence people. And before we go out there and exert our influence in the marketplace, we want to make sure our heads and hearts are in the right place.

Part of what we do during Man Morning is read Scripture together. We'll then ask each other, "What do you see here?" It's never, "Oh, no, that's not right; you're interpreting that wrong." It's "What do you see?"

So we'll read a passage from the book of promises, and we may get thirty different views on what God is showing a person about his own life through that section of Scripture. But somebody will almost always walk out of there thinking, *Whoa, that's amazing!* And it will change his life.

If Man Morning were just a bunch of men focused on whipping each other with rules and regulations and behavior modification, it wouldn't be powerful. Instead, it's a bunch of men sharing the love, mercy, and grace of God with each other as a group, so that we can take that out to the marketplace.

It's really about intimacy. We are learning to relate to each other at an intimate level. Once these men see that level of intimacy at work in their lives, they can channel it into the way they do business. It has been life-changing for a lot of these guys. I know for a fact that men from our group have done things in the marketplace, acted with courage and honesty and integrity in ways that they normally wouldn't have if it hadn't been for our group cheering them on.

Without a close relationship, we never know where people are in their lives. We may *think* we know, but in truth, we don't know how many people may be on the verge of suicide, bankruptcy, or divorce. We are all masters of hiding the deepest secrets and desires of our hearts. The reason we don't know where people are in their lives is because they don't show us.

That's why, as business professionals, the most powerful tool we have is self-disclosure. And the way you start learning self-disclosure is by creating a space where it is safe for you to disclose—to be honest and vulnerable. If I'm around someone who I know is not going to judge me for my opinion or my behavior, but who will accept me for who I am, then I can be open about the things with which I'm struggling.

Let me tell you what success is *not*. Success is not hiding your limitations, trying to block out the fear or depression or anger—whatever it is you think you shouldn't be feeling.

Real success is being able to share what's really going on with someone who is not going to judge us and who will accept us for the way we are—someone who can walk with us so that we make it to the other side alive.

Success is not about making a list: "Here are the five things I need to do be happy." I'm not interested in lists. I'm interested in the real life of a man who has experienced failure. I'm interested in a man who can teach me how to walk through life holding my head up.

It's about courage—courage to speak the truth, courage to be wrong, and courage to say I'm sorry and to admit failure. It's about never giving up, always seeing the best in people, looking for the win-win, believing in others and yourself, taking responsibility, saying you are right, forgiving others and yourself, and realizing nothing is perfect.

In your own life, where do you need courage to be vulnerable?

18

INSURE YOURSELF

It's important to have a support system around you. I've got one. These are the people in my life who say, "Hey, Mike, good job. Keep going, man; you can do it." Even when I fail, they don't abandon me. "That's OK, man. Pick yourself up and do it again."

A support system isn't the same as a bunch of yes-men. These aren't people who do nothing but praise and flatter me. They're honest—sometimes brutally honest—when I mess up. I've got close friends and family who say, "OK, every time you step up to the plate and put your left foot forward, you strike out. Why don't you try putting your foot back and see what happens?"

We all need people like this around us.

It's like insurance. Insurance is basically a community of people, even if it's people you never meet. Insurance works because everybody gives $100 to the pot, and when one of the participants gets sick, he or she gets to take money out. Not everybody has to get sick at the same time; in fact, let's hope that doesn't happen. But when you get sick, there's money waiting for you. Maybe you never take it out, but that's OK because you're insuring against something that could happen in the future.

We insure our cars, our houses, our health, and our lives. Why don't we insure ourselves with our own support systems? We aren't helping ourselves by being too proud to ask for help. It'll be far better if we can learn to say, "Hey, I'm not perfect. I need help."

But before you can feel safe doing that, you have to create a community of people who *can* and *will* help.

Remember, you're not the sun at the center of the solar system. Your community should not be all about other people revolving around you and responding to your every whim. You must give support to receive it. And stop complaining. The opposite of complaining is *encouraging*. Encourage others through their hard times, and they will encourage you.

There are two kinds of insurance you may be forgetting. There's relationship insurance, which is the support structure based on our true friendships. Because friendship is more important than our homes and cars. And then there's God insurance, which guarantees us eternal life—an eternal relationship with the only one who can give it.

Why is it that we insure every asset we own but fail to insure ourselves?

19

DOING THE DRILL

When I was growing up on the South Side of Chicago, my grandfather lived with us. One of his hobbies was carpentry. He'd go down to the basement, and I'd sit with him for hours, watching him build all kinds of things out of wood.

"Grandpa, what can I do to help?" I asked one day, wanting to be his little helper.

"Well, Michael, go fetch me the drill."

So I ran over to Grandpa's workbench, which was huge. You know how it is when you're a kid: everything is larger than life. There were tools all over the place. I looked around for the drill, then ran back and asked, "Grandpa, what's a drill?"

He smiled at me.

"You know how on Saturday nights we watch *Gunsmoke* with Matt Dillon?"

"Sure, Grandpa." *Gunsmoke* was cool, and Matt Dillon wasn't scared of anything. He was the kind of guy I wanted to be.

"You know the gun he carries?" Grandpa asked.

"Yes, sir."

"The drill looks like that gun."

So I ran back over to Grandpa's workbench and looked around some more. Finally, I found a tool that looked to me a lot like a gun.

I grabbed it, ran back to Grandpa, and exclaimed, "Here it is!"

He squinted at me and shook his head.

"Michael, that's a hammer."

At that point, Grandpa took me by the hand and walked me over to the workbench, where he pointed at the drill and said, "That's a drill."

My eyes got so big, looking at that thing. I was thinking, *Man, that's not a drill; that's an AK-47!* He even let me hold it while he was working, so I strapped it to my chest like a soldier. That's always been my picture of a drill.

Fast-forward about thirty years, when I had radial keratotomy done on my eyes—an operation performed to correct nearsightedness. Today they do it with a laser, but back then, they did it with a scalpel. So they made these incisions in my eyeballs, and a couple of weeks later, I was out on the golf course playing a round. I was having a lot of fun when, all of a sudden, something got inside my eye and I couldn't get it out. It was killing me, scratching my eye like sandpaper, and I was thinking, *I've ruined my eye. I'm going to go blind.*

I went to the doctor as soon as I could, and he put me under his scope to check out my eye.

"Mike," he said, "you have a tiny, microscopic piece of metal dust in one of the slits in your eyes, but it's nothing to be worried about."

"Easy for you to say, Doc!" I said. "I'm dying here."

"We can do one of two things," he told me. "We can wait, because in a couple weeks, it'll work itself out. Or, if you want, we can drill it out."

Now what picture of a drill do you think came to my mind when he said this? I was thinking of that drill I'd grown up with as a child: the AK-47 on my grandpa's workbench! I was picturing some kind of soldier in a white coat, drilling my eye out. I didn't think I'd ever be able to see again.

So I shared this story with the doctor, and we both had a laugh.

"No, Mike," he said. "*This* is a drill." And he pulled out this tiny little thing called an ophthalmologic drill. It looked like a toothpick with a little buffer cloth on top of it.

One word, "drill," and we had two totally different mental pictures. I had this specific picture from my childhood, while he was imagining something completely different. We were both looking through invisible filters—mine, from my experience as a kid, and his, from years of medical school and extensive training in the field. But when our filters were so diametrically opposed, it's no wonder we had some miscommunication!

If you've ever had a disagreement with a colleague at work, you probably know what it's like to look at an issue through very different filters. Maybe you and a coworker are working on the company's annual report, and you just can't see eye-to-eye on anything. Or you're presenting a new idea in front of the board, and you're frustrated that your co-presenter seems to be focusing on all the wrong things.

Let's say you've been assigned to a committee tasked with updating your company's "vision and values" statement. The committee is an eclectic group, running the gamut from a twenty-two-year-old recent college graduate gunning for more power in the organization to the white-haired director of marketing who has been with the company for thirty-five years. You'd better believe you're going to be dealing with some drastically diverse filters around that table! Even common business words like "vision" and "values" are going to be perceived differently. You might get so hung up on what the word "value" means that you spend the first hour arguing about it before you even get to the point of the meeting.

For us to do business, it's crucial that we learn to listen for—and look through—other people's filters before jumping to conclusions. I know it's hard to believe, but your opinion might not be the absolute truth. Of course, it's human nature to privilege our own filters. The minute we get into an argument with someone, we tend to think, *It's your fault! If you weren't who you are, I wouldn't be having a problem right now. If you could change who you are, my life would be easier.*

That's not the way to enter into a disagreement with someone, and it's *never* the way to settle one. It's far better to think, *Let me try and understand why you're thinking and feeling the way you are. Let me stand where you're standing and look through your filter.* Once we develop the habit of looking through other people's filters, we start to get why they're saying what they're saying.

So that's a fundamental step to having productive, healthy relationships with other people. We have to look through their invisible filters.

Step two is to go back to our own filters and think, *Why does it bother me when she says this or when he does that? What's going on with me?* That's humility, being able to identify our *own* hang-ups.

So, really, it's a two-prong process.

First I'm going to try to understand life through your filters, based on your life experiences, which are obviously different than mine. Then I have to step back and recognize my own filters for what they are: not the absolute truth and maybe not even true at all.

The third step is to look at the situation through God's filter. God has a powerful filter of love. When you have a conflict with somebody, here's what you could say: "You want to solve this right now? I know I do. Let's look at what Christ did for us, because both of us are forgiven for all our sins."

When you look at what Christ did on the cross, the ingredients of acrimony and conflict start to dissolve. God put His only Son on the cross to die for *our* sins. He did it because He loved us so much. To look through God's filter of love and compassion—now, *that* will inspire some humility.

I'm not saying you have to downplay your intellect. We want to use our intellect, especially in business, to get to the point where we can look at ourselves. We don't want to use it against each other or as a tool to wound one another. Whether you have a PhD, an MBA, or a good old-fashioned MRS, the real purpose of those fancy letters is simply to get to the point where we have humility in dealing with each other. I want to be able to see life through your eyes, then look at myself and ask, "Why am I feeling this way? Lord, what do you need to change in me so that I can understand what this person is going through?"

Sometimes you have to call a fig a fig. But sometimes you *can't* call a drill a drill, because words and ideas don't mean the same thing to everyone.

We all see the world differently, based on our past. What makes people so beautiful is that we come from such a broad range of backgrounds and have such varied life experiences. And with every unique person comes a unique set of filters. The better we get at looking through those human filters, the better we see the people we live and work with through God's abiding filter of love.

But what if you are dealing with someone who has no faith at all, or a different faith? Doesn't matter. Respect for another human being trumps anyone needing to be or feel right. What you believe about God should never negate love, humility, and respect toward each other.

What group of people do you find difficult to respect?

Part IV

THE OBSTACLE COURSE

♥ | 💰

20

THE FIVE INTERNAL TERRORISTS

We hear a lot about terrorism today. It seems like everyone is glued to his or her TV or computer screen, scrolling for news of the latest terrorist attack. One reason we are so sucked in by the idea of terrorism is that it makes us feel completely helpless. We never know where, when, or why an attack might come. We don't even know who's doing the attacking. And in the grips of fear, it's hard to move forward and live our lives.

The same can be said for the five internal terrorists, the ones we carry with us into our jobs, our marriages, and pretty much every interaction we have with others. They paralyze and inhibit us, poisoning our relationships and severely limiting what we're capable of.

Fear, judgment, pride, doubt, and lack of forgiveness—these are the five internal terrorists. They terrorize us daily, hourly. They are the enemies of success.

We rarely talk about these terrorists with others. Why? Because we're too busy trying to live our own lives to be concerned with how others live theirs. We are so busy fighting our own internal terrorists that we don't realize that everyone is fighting the same battle.

But what if you come to understand that you've been forgiven for everything—for every tiny thing you've ever screwed up in your life, from the beginning to the end? That God can free you of the terrorism perpetuated by fear, judgment, pride, doubt, and lack of forgiveness? How would you live then?

"Do not fear because I am with you," God says. "Do not anxiously look about you. I am your God. I will strengthen you. I will help you. I will uphold you. I am with you. I have given you my spirit. I have forgiven you. My view of you is what counts. My view of you is what will save you. My view of you is more important than seven billion human beings saying something. And when you grasp that, you'll know it's not what you do; it's who I am."

There's no way the five internal terrorists can stand up to that. God's words completely obliterate them. There's nothing left.

When we realize God's love and forgiveness—how our identity is in Jesus Christ—it will transform every area of our life. We will love our spouse. We will help people in need. We will get rid of fear and judgment toward others, in the same way that God has eradicated it for us.

We won't be consumed by doubt or pride, and we will treat everyone with forgiveness. The internal terrorists will no longer beat us because we know who we are and what we've been given.

Take that into the business world. Carry it with you into the high-stress atmosphere of conducting a transaction. You're sitting down in a boardroom, across from the vice president, trying to get him to do business. Your palms are sweating and inside, you're a nervous wreck. Now imagine what it would be like to be in that boardroom *without* fear (*I'll never get this deal*), judgment (*He's such a jerk; he won't treat me fairly*), pride (*He'd be crazy not to sign since I'm the best there is*), doubt (*I shouldn't even be here; this was a mistake*), or lack of forgiveness (*He passed me over for a promotion last year and I still resent him for it*).

What would that be like?

Now you're relating to the VP with confidence as a human being. You're just two people getting to know each other. You're not afraid you're going to lose. You're not afraid that someone is going to screw with you. You're not afraid to fail, because that familiar fear isn't with you anymore.

As a result, you can be real. You can sit in front of this guy and say, "Hey, I really want to win this opportunity.

I know you've got other people and I know we're trying to do this together. And in the past, I would have been sitting here thinking, 'Oh my God, I have to have this.' I just want you to know I'm very grateful to have this opportunity to sit in front of you and share with you, and I'm open to learning from you. I hope you will show me some things."

Can you imagine what the business world would look like if this were how people had conversations? How different would it be without the five internal terrorists silently holding a knife to everyone's throat?

21

DON'T BE A GRASSHOPPER

People are a lousy source of truth for themselves.

Someone told me that once, and man, did it stick with me! Oftentimes, the perspective I have of myself is just plain wrong. And if I think I know how others view me, I've got another thing coming.

It's almost funny how wrong we can be about others' perspectives of us. I might be speaking to a roomful of people, thinking, *Everybody in here hates me!* and then fifty people come up to me afterward to thank me for what I said. Or maybe I'm all high and mighty, feeling like I've got it all figured out, and I catch people throwing each other sideways looks, thinking, *What's with this guy? He can't tell his elbow from his rear end!*

We have a lot more influence than we think we do when it comes to what people believe about us. We can do ourselves a real disservice, or we can create an identity that makes buy-in easy. The choice is ours. We can influence the way others see us, based on *the way we see ourselves.*

Early in God's Word there's a story of twelve spies who went to check out the land of Canaan. All twelve spies couldn't believe what they had seen in Canaan: oranges the size of grapefruits, abundant fields of grain and veggies. It was a "land flowing with milk and honey," meaning, the prosperity of the region was amazing. It was all going well . . . until they saw the people living there.

They were giants. We're talking seven and eight feet tall. The Nephilim was a race of very big people. Ten of the twelve spies said, "Oh my goodness, look at the size of these guys! And look at us! They've got at least two feet on us, *and* they have weapons made of iron. We can't beat these guys. There's no way."

The Israelite reconnaissance team was full of fear. Even after the Creator of the universe led them through the desert and out of Egypt, showing them miracle after miracle after miracle, they had little faith.

Joshua and Caleb were the sole dissenters. "What do you mean?" they said. "We have God! Their size means nothing, because they don't have our God."

So all twelve spies came home to Israel and said their piece. But what the ten said was powerful. The ten spies talked about seeing the Nephilim, the native people of Canaan: "We seemed like grasshoppers in our own eyes," the spies said, "and we looked the same to them." The Nephilim were giants, and the ten spies had felt tiny in comparison!

Whom do you think the people listened to: the ten or the two? Fear is a powerful emotion; it can take root in the human heart more easily than courage. That's right; the ten spies instilled their fear in the rest of the nation. The Israelites, God's chosen people, saw themselves as grasshoppers—and so the rest of the twelve tribes of Israel saw themselves as grasshoppers too.

The ten spies came back home utterly convinced the Nephilim had seen them as little tiny bugs. But who'd told them that? Had they sat down and had a discussion with the natives of Canaan? No! Remember, they were there in secret, spying on the land. The giants hadn't said they were tiny! It was the way they saw themselves. In other words, the way the Israelites viewed themselves had given the Nephilim permission to view them in the same way. In fact, it gave all of Israel permission to view them as grasshoppers.

As businesspeople, what perspective do we have of ourselves? How do we present as we walk out our door and into the marketplace?

Depending on the perspective we have of ourselves, we either empower or disempower the people we work for and with. If we do not think we are valuable, we let others say bad things about us and mistreat us. It's our choice to either agree with them, or to stand up and say, "You know what? I'm a valuable person. Let's sit down and talk through this until we can see eye-to-eye."

Lead with courage.

That's what it takes to be a leader—not being afraid to be in the minority. If we want to succeed in business, we cannot allow ourselves to be guided by fear, even if our competition is fierce and much bigger than we are. We have to be like the two spies, Joshua and Caleb, who said, "It doesn't matter how big our enemies are. We've got God. We can't lose." These two men were not afraid to stand up to the other ten.

Right believing produces right behavior. What are we afraid of, anyway? Embarrassment? Failure? Disgrace? That stuff is not big. Fear causes us to behave a certain way, but so does faith. And I guarantee you, in business as in life, if you're running on fear, you're running on fumes. But if you have even a tiny mustard seed of faith? You will be able to move mountains.

Maybe you're sitting there thinking, *Nah, Mike, not me. I'm not the mountain-moving type.* That's when I remind you that you are a lousy source of truth for yourself. With God at your back, you *can* move mountains. And no, you probably won't be picking up the Rockies. But you are more than capable of facing down a dozen challenges every day, whether it means marshaling a new team of people or meeting an insane deadline. You may *think* you're a grasshopper, but God doesn't. And fortunately for you, God's Word always wins.

What does He say about what you think about most?

22

STOP HIDING

We all hide—each and every one of us. We hide from our spouses, we hide from our friends, we hide from our employers. We even hide from ourselves. It's really sad. We don't want people to see the way we really are, because we feel that if they do, they may not want to hang around with us.

Imagine the following scenario: One of your coworkers stands up at the next company meeting. He's sweating bullets. "I have to share something with you guys," he says. "I've been stealing from the supply closet. It's mostly little things—pens and paper and ink cartridges—but I know that doesn't make it right. I've also been calling in sick when I'm not sick. The truth is, I'm depressed. I don't know how I'm going to provide for my family from one day to the next."

He takes a deep breath.

"I know I'm going to get fired, and I deserve it. I don't blame you all for hating me; I deserve that too. I just don't want to hide anymore."

I'm guessing most of the people around that conference table would be horrified. They'd gasp and shake their heads.

But what about you? Ask yourself if you would have the courage to say the following to your coworker. "God bless you for coming out in the open and getting this off your chest. You've obviously been carrying it around for a while. It doesn't justify what you did, but doesn't it feel better to be honest? I'm sorry some of these guys want to judge you and put you in a box."

It took a lot of guts for your coworker to stand up and say what he said. And then we judge him for it? Why? God doesn't judge him for it. God knows every one of that guy's sins, every theft and lie he's told, and if the man has accepted Christ, God has already forgiven him for everything.

We hide behind the things we construct in our lives. Take another look around that conference room. What kind of walls have your coworkers built around themselves so that others can't see them the way they really are? Maybe they don't all steal from the supply room, but which of them are cheating on their spouse? Which of them lied on their résumé to get this job? Which of them are misusing company time by responding to personal email messages and placing Amazon orders while they're on the clock?

Now look at your boss. What is *he* hiding? Here's something no one talks about: If you've got a lot of money, you get to buy more props. Your buildings are higher; your walls are thicker. You've got security guards on top of the walls, and nobody can get close to you because you've got enough money to insulate yourself.

I'll tell you a secret: real freedom is living an insulation-free life.

That doesn't mean you tell every human being you meet every sin you've ever committed. "Hi, I'm Mike. I'll take a double espresso, please. And can you put in a little milk? Oh, and by the way, I cheated on my taxes. I dipped into the company till. I watched porn all last night. I just wanted to share that with you because I had to get it off my chest." That's not what I'm saying.

I'm saying that it pays to be vulnerable around the people you trust.

It's freeing to not hide. The stuff you hide will get ahold of you, and before long, it will control you.

We come from a long lineage of hiding. Our ancestors, Adam and Eve, hid from God. Then they hid from themselves in their shame and blaming. Ever since then, we've been hiding from each other. But it's time to come out of hiding. And it's time to stop judging other people when they do the same.

Isn't that true freedom?

23

TURNING A MESS INTO A MESSAGE

As businesspeople, we want our employers, employees, and colleagues to think we've got it all under control. We are desperate to appear cool, confident, and collected—like we already know everything and don't need anyone to do us any favors. We're terrified of messing up, so we work tirelessly to make others perceive us as perfect and faultless. But we don't do *ourselves* any favors by perpetuating this lie.

Nobody is perfect, and nobody knows everything. How could we? Human beings know an infinitesimal fraction of the knowledge in the universe. And yet we're still stubborn and headstrong, determined not to fail, or at least determined to make it look like we're not failing.

I'm going to tell you right now: *Fail.* If at first you don't succeed, keep failing. Fail and fail again. Fail publicly, epically, loudly. You should never be afraid to fail.

Failures are not to be feared or avoided. Failures are to be experienced!

The older you get, the more rich and deep your life experience, and the stronger your message becomes. Twenty-year-olds don't have that message yet, because it comes with age. By the time you get to fifty or sixty, you've started to articulate it.

The truth is that it's the mess you make in life that determines your message. If you never screw up, you won't have much of a message! All those failures and all that mess will produce a beautiful thing. Don't be afraid of it. The more you fail, the more you'll be able to share your message with other people, especially the people you mentor who are younger (and less experienced) than you. When I mentor a young man or woman, I often find myself saying, "Let me tell you the mess I got into as I aged, and here's what I learned from it."

Every human being on the planet has experienced failure after failure, but we all get a choice as to what we do with it.

We can take our mess and our failures and start to blame and criticize. We can make up myriad reasons why we failed. "If my parents were different, I wouldn't be like this." "If my colleague hadn't been five minutes late to our presentation, we would have closed that deal. He not only disrespected me; he also ruined this opportunity for me, and now I look bad to the partners. I'll never trust him again."

Or, we can say, "My colleague has a sick little girl. He could have chosen to miss the entire meeting, but he left his daughter and his wife at the hospital and tried like hell to make it here on time to support me. He must really care about this project and respect all the time and work I've put into it. And yeah, we didn't get this deal—but there's probably an even better one waiting just around the corner."

Which road do we take? Which road do *you* want to walk down in life?

If our failures reaffirm for us that we're not good enough, then the failures aren't doing what they're supposed to do. Our messes are our teachers. When we were kids, we had teachers in math and English and writing. When we got older, we had teachers that taught us how to think. But who teaches us how to feel? Who teaches us how to process failure? Who teaches us all that stuff?

Life does. And what do we do with that teacher when it comes to us? Do we use it as a building block, or do we play the blame game?

If, after being the number one salesman for twenty years, I'm suddenly not the number one salesman, I could respond by blaming the head of sales for "making a huge mistake" or spreading vicious rumors about the new leader. But why would I waste all that misspent energy?

For me, I'd much rather try to figure out why I'm no longer at the top. What am I learning? What choices am I making? How am I relating to others? What do I have to do to get back on top?

24

SOMETIMES YOU'VE GOTTA FALL ON YOUR FACE

A few years ago, I was in Las Vegas to talk to an insurance company. I hadn't been to Vegas in a long time, and when I walked into the Venetian, I couldn't believe it. The ceilings were huge, with these massive Michelangelo-style frescoes. This place was ostentatious.

I was speaking to the company that night; at eight o'clock I would walk into the ballroom and speak to roughly six hundred people. I was excited. I had just lost my mom, and I found myself thinking, *Mom, I wish you were here. I mean, I'm talking in Vegas.* My name wasn't in lights or anything, but it was cool, and I wished she could have experienced it with me.

So I entered the ballroom and was really feeling the energy. They'd hired a guy named Ned to do all their audio-visual, and he was standing in the back.

"Hey, Ned," I said. "Do you mind if I run down the aisle when you announce me?"

He blinked.

"You want to do what?"

"I want to run down the aisle. You know, you'll announce me and I'll start running. I used to work for IBM in Poughkeepsie, and we'd have to run into the classroom every morning with a white shirt and tie on, singing an IBM song. So I figured it would be kind of cool if I ran down the aisle tonight."

Ned shrugged but radioed it in to his colleague: "When you play the music, Mike is going to run down the aisle."

So I got all wired up, and I was pumped. What I didn't know was that when they put the music on, which was the theme song from *Rocky,* they would turn the lights off. The ballroom had those big crystal balls with strobe lights, so every three seconds I could see where I was going. But those were some *long* seconds in between. I couldn't see the carpet. I couldn't see anything at all.

So I started running and I got about halfway, and all of a sudden, I was Superman. My whole life flashed before my eyes. I was suspended in midair, thinking, *Mike, this was your idea. Nobody told you to run down the aisle. You did this on your own. Now you're going to fall down and hit the carpet. And you know what? There's nothing you can do about it.*

Sure enough, I hit the carpet. Hard. There was a big explosion via the microphone. They stopped the music and turned on the lights while I was lying there. So I got up and ran back to where I'd started.

"What are you doing?" Ned hissed.

"I just fell!"

"You've got to get back out there."

He radioed to his colleague, "Play the music again."

"Go, Mike. Go!"

So I started running again. And they turned the lights out again! For the second time! I couldn't believe it. The light was hitting the strobe and I fell in the exact same spot. I was face down on the carpet yet again!

Self-defeating thoughts were racing through my mind. I was finished. I was going to get up and walk right past them, get my clothes, go to the airport. I'd be the talk of the town that night—maybe for a few days; then they'd all forget about me. But I didn't care.

And then these arms grabbed me from behind. They picked me up, hoisting me off the carpet, until I was standing on my feet. It was Ned.

"Come on, Mike," he said. "I'll run with you." And he ran with me all the way to the front.

We got on stage, and Ned turned me around. Everyone applauded. The whole ballroom had seen me fall, not once, but twice. Ned's colleague turned the lights back on and I was facing 1,200 eyeballs. I was standing there, thinking, *Oh boy. Here we go.* I had to think fast.

"Have you ever in your life planned something out and did it the best you knew how?" I asked the crowd. "You were never going to get a divorce. You were going to make all this money. You were going to make a big entrance by running into a ballroom of six hundred people." A few chuckles. "That was the way your life was going to turn out: no problems. And then you fell flat on your face? Can anybody relate to that?"

People nodded.

"Ned, get me a microphone," I said, and he did. "Anybody want to share their story?" I asked the group.

A guy tentatively raised his hand. I brought him the mic, and he started talking. He shared a personal tale about a time he'd fallen flat on his face at work.

Then somebody else said, "Hey, let me share." We had about five people share their stories.

When they were done, I addressed the crowd.

"Do you realize that we've just connected on our woundedness? We just connected on our insecurities and our fears in life. That's what connects people. Not our successes, not the battles we've won, not our résumé, not 'I'm better than you.' Not all this stuff on the exterior that we use to separate ourselves from one another. It is our woundedness and being honest about our failures that connect us on a real, human-to-human level.

"And you know what? I feel more comfortable standing up in front of you having fallen on my face two times in front of you and saying, 'I fell. I screwed up. And now you have to listen to me for an hour.'" They laughed. "But now I'm listening to some of you, too, and it's drawn us all closer together."

Today I find myself in the marketplace among peers. These are salespeople and CEO-level colleagues, people who have positions and titles. The question becomes: How can I connect, human to human, with these people? And what I've learned is that I have to be the one to self-disclose first. I have to be willing to fall flat on my face. Why? Because that opens people up.

How do we step out of these protective shells we've spent our whole lives developing? Easy. We share our woundedness and failures. We self-disclose our fears and imperfections. We aren't afraid to fall, fail, and screw up.

It may seem counterintuitive to everything you've ever learned about business, but sometimes you just have to fall flat on your face.

When this happens again, what will be your next step?

Part V

BUSINESS GRACE

♥ | 💰

25

LORD, HAVE MERCY

You're working late. You think the office is deserted, but as you're heading out, you notice the lights are still on in the conference room. Curious as to which of your colleagues is burning the midnight oil, you go to investigate. You're surprised to find Alex, your assistant, hunched over the conference table, crying. Alex looks up at you and says, "I messed up. I did something I shouldn't have."

What is your first response? Do you feel angry and judgmental, assuming Alex probably screwed up something important? Do you want to go rat Alex out to your boss so that justice can be served? Or do you move to compassion and mercy?

Before you answer that, I want to tell you a story.

A man lost his wife in a tragic car accident and was raising his seven-year-old son by himself. He worked hard all week to put food on the table, but on the weekends, he always took his son to the park.

There was an orphan boy who hung out at the park too. He'd started to notice the man and his son. He'd watch them stroll into the park together, the dad holding his little boy's hand, and then, together, they'd sit down on a bench.

One day, he heard the father say, "Son, go play. I'll watch you."

The orphan boy watched as the son scampered up the ladder and shouted from the top, "Daddy! Daddy! Watch me!" Then he'd fly down the slide, and his dad would smile. The little boy would do the same thing on the monkey bars, the swing set, the merry-go-round— and every time, the boy's dad would beam and smile and cheer.

The orphan boy saw all that love and thought, "I wish *I* had that." He was jealous.

So one day, the little orphan boy climbed up behind the man's son on the slide. He waited until he was sure the father wasn't watching, then pushed the seven-year-old boy hard off the ladder. The little boy fell and broke his neck. His father rushed him to the hospital, but even the doctors couldn't save him. The little boy died.

But the orphan boy was wrong: The father *was* watching. He saw everything. He knew exactly what had happened to his son. And now one of three things could happen.

The first is *judgment*. The father could take revenge. He could go back to the park and wait for the orphan boy to climb up on the slide, then push him off the ladder. The father, in his anger and his grief, could decide that what had happened to his son is going to happen to this kid too. "An eye for an eye, a tooth for a tooth." Judgment equates punishment.

The second is *justice*. The father could go to the authorities and say, "I know the kid who did this to my son. He threw my little boy off the slide and killed him. What are you going to do about it?" He could go through the due process of law that we've set up in our society. The father could depend on the criminal justice system to punish the orphan boy to the full extent of the law: putting him in juvie, assigning community-service hours, etc.

But there's a third way too. This third way is what the father chooses. It's called *mercy*.

He takes the orphan boy home and raises him as his own son. The boy takes the son's room and sleeps in the son's bed. The bereaved father teaches him how to love and how to live. He teaches him everything he's learned since losing his son. Now *that's* mercy.

We don't see a lot of mercy in business. But that's the heart of our Father in Heaven. My God is full of compassion and mercy, and that's the way He treats people. Mercy is His default.

But how do we treat people with mercy in business? Especially when we get kicked down and lied to and deceived? Let's say Alex is *my* assistant and has been lying to me for weeks about a deal I'd thought was in the bag. The truth is: the deal didn't actually go through because Alex didn't do due diligence and has been scared to death to tell me the truth. Do I respond with mercy, even though I've lost what was rightfully mine?

Heck no! I don't get mad; I get even, right? I tell myself it's all about justice; I'm doing the right thing by ensuring that my assistant gets fired immediately. I want to expose Alex so that this never happens again.

Don't get me wrong; sometimes that's what has to be done. You can't run a business on the backs of thieves and liars. But there are also times when you can choose mercy. You can take a candid look at what's really going on. You feel small, you feel stupid, you feel entitled to whatever you thought you should get and now aren't getting—and realize that you're not acting out of "justice." You're acting out of your own wounded ego. You're responding from a place of judgment, not compassion—and certainly not love.

Now are there times when we might need to take a hard line about something? Of course. I'm asking us to consider both sides when looking at a situation.

Every time you feel angry at work, every time you feel the urge to "get even," ask yourself the following questions: How can I be merciful? How can I be kind, fearless, and nonjudgmental? How can I put aside pride and choose forgiveness instead?

It's difficult, but it can be done. If we could all learn how to choose mercy, I suspect it would change the way we do business. It would change the way we do life.

How would choosing mercy change how you do business? Be specific.

26

STARTING AT THE FINISH LINE

A guy is training for the summer Olympics in the 100-meter freestyle. He's training so he can compete against every nation in the world, the very best swimmers from over a hundred countries. This guy wants the gold medal. He wants to be the very best there is.

So every day, he gets up at six o'clock in the morning and goes down to the pool to meet his coach. He swims all day, and he does this seven days a week—for four years. He practices some other strokes but focuses mainly on freestyle. His coach measures how much food he eats because he's got to have a certain amount of protein intake balanced with a certain amount of fats and carbohydrates. And so this guy is monitored perfectly. They look at his body fat. They analyze his stroke in the pool. This young guy is scrutinized by every machine that can scrutinize an athlete.

In the evening, he goes home. All he talks about with his family is swimming and the Olympics and his chance of taking home gold. And when he's walking down the street, everybody looks at him and thinks, *That's the guy who's going to represent the United States in the Olympics!* I mean, this guy breathes it, lives it, and sleeps it. All he can think about is that gold medal. And he does this every single day for four years, all in the hopes that in a couple-minute swim he will win an Olympic gold medal.

Now, let's say that before he started all that training, he gets a knock on his door, and it's some members of the Olympic Committee.

They say to him, "Are you so-and-so?"

And he replies, "Well, I guess I am."

"Can we come in?" they ask. "We're from the Olympics."

Of course he lets them in. They all sit around the coffee table, and the woman who seems to be in charge pulls out a gold medal, which she puts around his neck.

Obviously, he's astonished.

"What are you doing?" he asks.

"We're giving you the gold medal for the 100-meter freestyle," she says.

"But I haven't done anything yet. I haven't even started training!"

"That's OK. We know you deserve it."

The guy is starting to get agitated.

"You don't understand," he says. "I have not done anything. I want to train for four years. I want to prove to the American public how good I am. I want to perform against every nation on the planet. I want to *earn* that gold medal. You're not even giving me an opportunity to prove myself!"

The woman shrugs and says, "You're the best. You know it; we know it. We're going to give you the gold medal anyway."

Now let me ask you a question: Where's the incentive to win if, before you even start, before you even begin training, you are handed the gold medal?

Here's another example. Let's say I'm a commission salesman. Everything I do is 100-percent commission; I don't get a salary, so if I don't sell, I don't eat. Imagine that I am trying to sell this $5 million transaction to an oil company, and it's going to take me about a year to make the sale. I'll get a commission of $50,000 if, after the year is out, I make this sale.

So I drive down to the oil company and start doing all the things I'm supposed to do to make the sale. I get to know all the decision makers. I want to know what they like to do and what they don't like to do, what they're looking for in a product and what they're not looking for. I want to know my competition better than they know themselves. I take my clients out to lunch and dinner; I wine and dine them. I even take them golfing.

In fact, I don't just want to get to know them; I want to get to know their wives, their kids, and their grand-kids. I memorize their birthdays. I learn every single thing I can so that when I present my product to the board of directors, they'll make a decision in my favor. I want them to like me. I do everything within my power to win this sale.

Now, let's say that before I start this whole process, I go to get my mail and there's a letter from my company. I open the letter and inside, there's a check for $50,000. I take one look at it and immediately call my company up and ask for the payroll department.

"There must be a mistake," I say. "I just got a check for $50,000."

They transfer me to the company president who says, "That's no mistake, Mike! That's the commission for the $5 million sale you're going to close in a year."

"But I haven't done anything yet," I say. "I haven't even made my first call on the company!"

"That's OK," he says. "You're going to get the deal. You know it; we know it. We want to pay you up front."

It's the same deal as with the athlete: I haven't been given the opportunity to prove myself. So where's the incentive? If I receive the reward up front—the money, the medal, whatever—where will the drive come from for me to go out and do my job?

It feels so counterintuitive.

And yet, this is exactly what God does with us. He starts us at the finish line. When a person puts his trust in Jesus Christ—in His death, burial, and resurrection— God forgives our sins, changes our heart, and gives us eternal life and the gift of the Holy Spirit. It happens right then. He takes away all our sin, approves of us, and accepts us perfectly and completely at the very moment we put our trust in Him. We haven't even had an opportunity to obey Him yet, and He starts us out with everything up front.

Now that's good news.

But wait, what's the incentive for us to live a Christian life? To live a life that is pleasing to God? I'll tell you what our incentive is: it's changing our view of God.

When we become aware of what God has really offered us at the cross, it changes the way we view Him. This can only happen when we see our Lord in Heaven not only as the Creator of the entire universe, a being worthy of our awe and respect, but also as our father and our friend.

I have a pastor friend in Chicago who could not get his young daughter to obey him. He'd tried every-thing: punishing her, taking away her toys, sending her to time-out. Nothing worked. She just kept being rebellious. So here's what he did. He told me about his unorthodox approach and I'll never forget it.

The pastor called his daughter, Tammy, down into his study.

"Sweetheart, come on in," he said. So she stepped tentatively into his study and saw that her father was standing there with one of those fourteen-inch gold, metal rulers.

Tammy became very pale.

"Oh no, Daddy, please don't hurt me."

"Close the door, Tammy," he said. "I'm not going to hurt you."

So she closed the door and walked over to him, trembling.

Then her dad did something surprising: he took the ruler and handed it to her. He balled his hands into fists and held out his arms in front of her.

"Now, Tammy, I want you to hit me on the knuckles with that ruler."

"Daddy, I don't want to do that."

"Tammy," he said, "we are not going to leave this room until you hit my knuckles with that ruler."

So she took the ruler and mildly rubbed it against her father's knuckles.

"Hit me harder," he said.

Tammy's eyes filled with tears.

"Daddy, please, I don't want to do this."

In response, he made her hit his knuckles until they hurt.

By the end, she was sobbing.

"Daddy, I am so sorry. I don't want to do this. Don't make me do this. I'll never disobey you again, Daddy."

And he took her and put her in his lap, and he said, "Tammy, I love you. But this is what Jesus did. We're disobedient. We've sinned. And instead of punishing us, God took the punishment upon Himself. He bled for us so we wouldn't have to bleed."

That's the incentive. That little girl's incentive was: "I don't want to hurt my daddy because I know and love my daddy." And when we get to know God as a loving daddy, we're not going to want to hurt Him. We're going to want to follow Him because He knows what's best for us.

The incentive for the salesperson to receive the money up front? The incentive for the swimmer to receive the gold medal before even starting his process? That *is* the incentive. It starts from within, not for a prize at the end.

Are you competing after already having won or are you competing to win?

27

WHO OR WHAT DETERMINES SUCCESS

When I started out in sales years ago, I had one mantra. It was, simply: "I'm not gonna lose."

I remember a guy coming up to me at one of my events. I didn't know him well, but I knew he also worked in the sales department at my company.

"You've been number one for thirteen years in a row now, Mike," he said. "Next year, you'd better move over, because I'm gonna be the new number one."

The guy was standing there, earnest as can be, with his very pregnant wife on his arm. And I laughed. I actually laughed.

"What's so funny?" he asked.

"You can't beat me," I said. Suffice it to say I wasn't the most humble guy back then.

The guy looked me squarely in the face.

"You really believe that?"

Let me tell you what was going through my head at that moment. As he, himself, had just noted, I'd been the number one salesman with the company for the past thirteen years. My numbers came in extremely high every quarter. I was their number one guy from the late eighties all the way to the end of the nineties. We were printing money back then; that's how crazy this business was.

"I do believe that," I said, "and here's why. You've got a family, and come Christmas Eve, you'll be sitting under the tree, opening up gifts with your wife and new baby. A week later, you'll be celebrating the New Year with them. But I'll work Christmas Day. I'll work New Year's Eve. I'll work New Year's Day, because I can't lose. My identity is wrapped around whether I win or not. Yours isn't, which means I will do whatever it takes to win."

I could tell the guy and his wife were surprised by my candor. But I wasn't done yet.

"Imagine a guy from Tennessee who comes onto your college campus weighing 125 pounds. He's five foot eight, in good shape. There's also a 225-pound weightlifter front lineman for the football team—obviously, a bigger guy. But if that kid from Tennessee says, 'I can't lose a fight, even if I kill you,' I will put my money on him, not the bigger guy, because the bigger guy won't kill him. This guy will go all the way to the death. That's why that guy won't lose.

"It's the same with me in business. I can't be number two. So you can't win, because I'll do whatever it takes to be number one. I won't kill or cheat or steal, but I won't lose."

Looking back, it's hard for me to believe I said all that to the poor guy. I was ruthless. What I didn't know at the time was that I was at the beginning of a very long process of divorcing my success as a salesman from my worth as a human being.

In the years that followed, God showed me it wasn't about my being number one. I was already number one in His eyes. But for me to fully understand that, it would take many years of God saying, "I sent my Son to die for you, Mike. I'm your God. You're in right relationship with me. You and I are OK. We're at peace because of the cross. You don't have to strive to get people to like you. I already like you, and I'm a majority."

For years I fought with Him.

I said, "Wait a minute, God. What about all the hard work I did?"

"It doesn't mean you don't work hard, Mike. But you're number one to me, and it has nothing to do with some sales report. You're still number one, but think of it this way: now the stress of being number one is gone, just like the swimmer training for the Olympics."

What ways in your life are you obsessed with being number one? Do you want to be the number one spouse, parent, manager, or sales rep? What would happen if those titles were stripped away from you? Who would you be then?

Everybody wants to feel valuable—every single human being on the planet. We're all asking, "Am I worthwhile?" "Do I have value?"

For the first years of our lives, we get our value from our parents and siblings. Think about it. For at least five full years, we're stuck in a house with Mom and Dad, and we learn a lot from them—both from the way they relate to one another and the way they treat us, their child.

By the time you make it to first grade, you've already got a pretty solid narrative about your value as a person, whether that value is high or low.

Then you start going to school, and your teacher and classmates give their own estimation of your value. And you grow up and interact with other people in society, at schools and churches and companies and communities. You get older and go to college and make money and get married and have kids of your own, but the same dynamics are still at play. You're still searching for your worth as a human being. You're still asking, "Do I have value?"

As long as we allow the world to define us, we're trapped. We are forced to find something that gives us temporary value, and we had better not lose hope because if we do, we might as well kill ourselves. If our identity is wrapped up in "being number one," however we define it, and then we lose hope that we'll ever get there, it can feel like there's nothing left to live for.

If academia is the route you took to get your value, then failing to get that PhD in economics will make you feel like you've failed at life. If you define your worth by your holdings in the stock market and you're not a multimillionaire, you might think it's worth ending your life. You wouldn't be the first to conflate a market loss with a loss of value; tragically, suicides tend to rise as stocks fall.

But what if you could be number one *regardless* of your accomplishments? What if your value has nothing to do with how much money you make or the kind of car you drive, and has everything to do with God's abundant love? What if you believed that, no matter how many mistakes you make or failures you accumulate over your lifetime, you will still be number one?

Well, do believe it. Because In God's eyes, you already are.

That's starting at the finish line!

28

THAT GUY YOU LOVE TO HATE

No matter where you work, there's always "that guy" or "that girl," the one with whom you're constantly frustrated. This is the guy who's always standing in your way, blocking everything you want. You know the one I'm talking about. His face probably sprang to mind as soon as you saw the words "that guy."

Sometimes you find yourself praying things like, "Lord, I'm so mad at that guy! Can't you just get rid of him? Can't you make him get fired or downsized or whatever it takes? He's blocking everything!"

It's funny, but the word "mad" isn't even the right use of language. Mad means crazy. It's an adjective, a descriptive word. You can't be "mad" at somebody any more than you can be hungry or crazy at somebody. So when you say, "I'm mad," what you're actually saying is, "I'm crazy. The target for my craziness right now is that person."

When I say, "I'm mad at that guy, God; take him out," it's because I think he's blocking what I want. But what if that guy is actually a teacher? What if God wants to train me through that guy I can't stand?

If I'm a weightlifter who is serious about building muscle, I add resistance bands to my weights. You can get them pretty thick—eighty pounds of resistance. And if you're me, you're lifting weights and saying, "This is hard!" But that resistance is helping my muscles grow.

The obnoxious people in our lives are like resistance bands: they help us grow. But we don't like to hear that. We want to get rid of the resistance bands and make it easier for ourselves. We'd prefer that God "clean house" and take out all the people we'd rather not deal with. "Get rid of the resistance bands, God," we say.

But God's not going to do that. He's the one who put them there! If you want to grow, you've got to have those bands. If you're trying to get somewhere, you should welcome those resistance bands because they're going to help you reach so much higher than you could on your own.

The next time you find yourself griping about that guy or girl you love to hate, think of him or her as a resistance band. You may not like it, but that person is growing you, and you're only going to get stronger as a result.

Start asking yourself different questions, like, "What am I feeling because of this resistance, and why?" and "What can I learn or change about *myself*, not the other person?"

29

EVERY DAY OF THE WEEK

How do you stay true to God in the dog-eat-dog world of business? How do you follow Him when vicious office politics threaten to swallow you whole? How do you keep your head above water when you're trying to do things differently and you seem to be the only one?

We've all been to business seminars, right? You know the ones I mean. You emerge on Sunday afternoon into the bright light of day, still jacked up on adrenalin. You're going to set these goals and take these actions . . . and then Monday morning hits. Suddenly, you've got two hundred email messages in your inbox, and it's back to business as usual. Nothing has changed.

People want hope. Those business seminars will never lack for participants, because what they're selling is hope, and there will always be men and women who are starved for it. But most of the seminars are missing the foundational element.

They're missing God.

The gurus and motivational speakers make their millions by chanting, "You can do it!" They whisper into people's ears: "It's all about *you.* Get confident; go for the gold! You've got what it takes inside you to achieve all your dreams."

But nobody has "what it takes" inside of themselves. Sure, some people are stronger than others; some have more willpower or a thicker skin. But Jesus said, "Apart from me, you can do nothing." It's *not* all about you. Anyone who tells you that is feeding you a lie. It's about God.

But for some people, God should just stick to Sundays, where He belongs. Their attitude is, "Spirituality is something you do on Sundays. But from Monday to Friday, let's get real: you can't take that stuff into the office. You'll get killed."

And I won't lie to you; it can be hard.

How are you supposed to turn the other cheek when the guy you're negotiating with flat-out lies to you? When "turning the other cheek" could cost your company a million dollars? How do you walk out your passion for God in the workplace?

First off, let's define spirituality. Are we talking about a wishy-washy seventy-five-year-old who walks around handing out beads to people, saying, "I love you! God loves you"? Because, yeah, that person is probably not going to fare well if he has to turn around and negotiate a $5 million deal, and a competitor is tearing his throat out because he wants to get there first.

Jesus said, "Be as wise as serpents, but as innocent as doves." That doesn't mean we take our intellect and trash it. Not at all. We're not killing our intellect for God, because God doesn't want us to do that. In fact, that's the *last* thing He wants.

Let me give you an example from the life of a guy I used to work with. A few years ago, Bob was headed to a negotiating table because the company had hired him to go sell a product. The lease of the product was ending, and now this other guy wanted to buy it, and we were in the hole. Basically, the original product cost roughly $3 million. Even after all the lease payments they had given us, we were still a million dollars in the hole. So Bob had to get that money back somehow.

Our company was at the end of term. Bob was a million bucks in the hole, but he owned the product. The product had a street value of $300,000. If Bob's client did his homework, then maybe he'd offer $400,000— meaning, the company would lose $600,000. And we weren't in the business of losing that kind of money.

So Bob went in and talked to the client, and the client said, "We need to buy this stuff out."

Bob said, "Great!"

Now, Bob's a swell guy. He's full of God's love, and I have no doubt he loved the guy sitting in front of him. But this wasn't his employer; it was his client. And Bob had an employer who paid his salary—a.k.a., our boss. He had to listen to what our boss told him to do. His job description was to maximize profit for the corporation; that's why they'd hired him.

So now we were at a chess table with this client. And they started haggling.

Bob said, "I'm thinking $2.2 million; that would be a good price."

The client's eyes bugged out.

"2.2? Are you kidding me? No way we'd offer you more than a million for this!"

Now, he had just tipped his hand, right? Bob didn't even know what number he had been thinking, but now the guy had said a million. So Bob thought, *Great! Worst-case scenario, I break even.*

But to this guy, Bob said, "Come on, are you kidding me? A million dollars?! I'm going to have to get my attorney involved!"

They went back and forth, and Bob ended up selling the product for $2 million. He'd made the company a million dollars in profit. We were ecstatic. We were waving flags with his name on them. Because he had done his job: he'd maximized profit for the company. Now, the other guy hadn't checked the marketplace. If he had done so, he would have known that $2 million was incredibly inflated. But was that Bob's responsibility, to make sure he checked market value? Nope. That was the *client's* responsibility. He had a different employer than Bob did. Bob loved him; Bob was kind. That didn't change the fact that Bob worked for a company that was paying his salary and telling him to go out and maximize profit, which is exactly what he had done.

These dynamics happen every single day in business. Does it make you uncomfortable? Good! That means we're finally asking the right questions. How do we, as businessmen, engage in business with God in us, when at the same time, we've got to do our jobs?

Did Bob lie to the client? No, he never lied to him. The client never asked Bob what the fair market price was. There's so much gray area in business. It's very rarely black-and-white.

Does that mean God gets pitched out the door? Absolutely not. God is in all of us, which means I take Him everywhere I take myself. I take myself into my business. I take myself into Starbucks. I take myself home at night. I take myself to a grocery store. Wherever I go, God is with me. Now, can I turn that on and off? Can I become a jerk? Sure, at times! But am I living a double life? Am I one me on Sunday, and then a completely different me from Monday through Saturday? No. I'm the same me every day of the week.

If I have a Sunday life and a business life, it's because my view of God is still skewed. I think God is angry at me and pissed off. I didn't do it right. And because I'm guilty and ashamed, I feel like I have to disclose everything—every thought, feeling, and move I have ever made.

It's like when a job application reads, *List your last four jobs*, and some people feel so terrified and ashamed, they list absolutely everything. *I worked for two weeks at a hot dog stand, because I got fired from my last job . . . and then there were those three days when I didn't show up for work because I had another job.* That is not how you fill out a job application! It wasn't the applicant's honesty talking; it was the applicant's guilty conscience.

In the same way, doing the job your boss told you to do does not mean you are living a double life. On the contrary, it means you are being true to your purpose. Your bigger purpose is to let God show His love and compassion through everything you do. But that doesn't mean you can't also fulfill your purpose of doing a good job for your company.

The question is, does God love and live through you every day of the week?

Part VI

YOUR VIEW OF VALUE

♥ | 💰

30

THE PUPPY OR THE DIAMOND RING

"One man's trash is another man's treasure." We've all heard the expression. It simply means that something may be utterly worthless to one person, while it's the find of a century for another.

I once met a musician who made his instruments entirely out of other people's junk. He had fashioned elaborate guitars out of old PVC pipes, busted tin coffee pots, and bent wires. Where I saw broken pieces of trash, he saw music. You'd better believe when that man went to a junkyard, he saw the world very differently than I did!

Who sets *our* value? Who decides who is valuable and who isn't?

If we try to set our own value as humans, instead of accepting the inherent value each of us has been given by God, we are setting ourselves up for disappointment.

This is particularly true in business, where we become easily attached to external circumstances: how many sales we made for the company this year, when we last got promoted, the parking place with our name on it out front.

The more attached we get to our perceived value of ourselves, the more affronted we are when others' perceptions don't match up to our own. It can be a big challenge when we realize that an aspect of ourselves that we'd thought held great value isn't so valuable to someone else.

My friend Hank was raised in the jewelry business. His grandfather had opened up a store at the turn of the twentieth century in the glittering Jewelry District of Downtown Los Angeles. The store has been passed down from generation to generation, and has had quite a few celebrities pass through its doors. Hank understands life through the filter of a diamond and has always felt lucky to be able to assist people in buying beautiful gems for their loved ones.

A couple of years ago, Hank was invited to his son's school for Career Day. All the kids gathered around to listen to him talk about his job. Hank pulled a four-carat rectangular diamond in a cellophane bag from his pocket. The value of the diamond was $400,000 a carat. Essentially, he was carrying $1.6 million in his pocket. He was prepared to knock their socks off.

"Kids, this is a diamond. This is what I sell to your dad when your mom and dad get in a fight," he joked.

He passed the diamond around and watched anxiously as the kids pawed it with their sticky little hands. He monitored them closely, afraid that someone might mistake the diamond for a Flintstones vitamin and swallow his vast fortune. After they'd each had a chance to hold it, he began his planned presentation.

"Diamonds are made of carbon. The word comes from the ancient Greek, adámas, meaning "unbreakable," because diamonds are the most durable minerals— "

Something in the room shifted. Hank felt it immediately. He had lost their attention. The kids were gaping at the door, where another student's father was standing with a six-week-old cocker spaniel.

He put the diamond back in his pocket and made way for Joshua's father, who owned a pet shop. When Joshua's father walked in with the puppy, the kids went nuts. They jumped all over him, cuddling and squeezing him, petting his ears, pulling his legs, and fighting urgently over whom he liked the most. Hank sat at the back of the classroom, gripping his diamond. He was renowned throughout the city for his high-quality jewelry and couldn't believe he had failed to impress a group of six-year-olds.

After the excitement had died down and Joshua's father had joined Hank at the back of the classroom, the teacher returned to the front.

"Class, today you learned about two businesses," she said. "If you had all the money in the world, where would you rather shop?"

The answer was unanimous. Everybody wanted to buy the puppy. Even Hank's own son, the heir to the family business, chose the damn dog! Why? Because to them, the puppy was more valuable. Hank was crest-fallen. The diamond was just a shiny piece of glass, worthless in their eyes.

Any grown adult would pick the diamond over the puppy. I don't care how much you love animals; you could take the diamond and trade it in for five thousand kennels. Adults know the value that diamonds have in the marketplace. Kids value puppies because they're soft and adorable.

Who determines value? If the world were made up of seven billion children, it would cost thirty puppies to buy a BMW! We value the diamond because we know the ascribed worth of that jewel, the status of the diamond. And somebody's willing to pay $1.6 million to have that.

Can you determine the value of a person? Only someone greater than us can do that. You don't have enough power to set my value. I don't have enough power to set your value. You're a created product, just like me. That's like a chair trying to determine the value of another chair; it's stupid.

But this is what we do with each other all the time. We make judgments based on how much money someone has or what he has accomplished in his career. I'm here to tell you, that doesn't make any sense. If a person's value were really determined by his net worth, a four-year-old wouldn't have any value because he has never earned a dime. And ask any parent of a four-year-old: they're pretty sure that kid has tremendous value!

You have value because you were created in the image of God. I'm valuable because I breathe air. I walk. I think. I feel. I decide. I have a system of beliefs that guides me. And where does that come from? Not from my public world, by managing my image. Not from my professional world, by earning a lot of money or being promoted to the C-suite. Not from my personal world, by watching my kid hit a home run.

Where does it come from? It comes from the fact that I know who I am because God put me on this planet to express Himself through my unique personality and talents.

Now, Hank's not a bad guy because he sells diamonds. Of course not—that's his job, his place in the professional world. And Joshua's father, who owns the pet store, isn't a better guy, even though the kids might think so. Their value as humans is not determined by how they make money.

If Hank had walked out of the school after his disappointing presentation and donated that rock to a charity, and if he had done it from a heart of love, and not guilt, his value would not have changed in the eyes of God, even though that would have been an amazing thing for him to have done.

Imagine what it would be like to live our lives *knowing* that nothing we achieve, accomplish, or perform (even giving away a $1.6 million diamond) will *ever* add to or take away from who we are at any one moment in time . . . from birth to death. What a feeling! That's freedom: to finally be free enough to give, forgive, trust, believe, and be kind . . . because you *know* the value you already possess and you needn't do or accomplish anything to add to that fact.

Do you think if we believed this, we would need fewer drugs to help us sleep and less TV to quiet our nerves, and we would have more love and tenderness to show our families and the rest of the world?

31

TREASURE IN A BROWN-BAG LUNCH

Treasures pop up where we least expect them.

When I was in grammar school, my favorite time of the year was the end of the first day. The teacher would give us a list of the stationery items we had to have for the school year. "You need three No. 2 pencils, six spiral notebooks, and tabs." We went through a complete list of everything we had to bring to school the next day. And that evening, Mom would take me to the stationery store to get all these items.

Picture a serious six-year-old walking down the aisle with this long list. I was militant about it. I would say to my mother, "Mom, they've got to be No. 2 pencils. They can't be No. 3; they *have* to be No. 2." I'd end up with a pocket organizer full of No. 2 pencils and BIC pens, and a whole stack of spiral notebooks. Everything had to be just right.

But my favorite part was the lunch-pail aisle.

Every year, Mom bought me a new lunch pail. One year, I had a lunch pail with a picture of Yosemite Sam on it, and it was my all-time favorite. His moustache wrapped around the entire pail.

So I'd have my lunch in my new lunch pail and I'd walk to school and we would compare lunch pails with one another. One of the guys I used to walk to school with had Batman and Robin; another guy had Archie from Archie Comics. But I'll never forget how, every single day at lunch, we would gather around the desk of a kid named Larry.

Larry, we all knew, came from a poor area of the South Side of Chicago. His family didn't have much and he couldn't afford a lunch pail. He would always bring a sack lunch, just a regular brown paper bag. Yet every day, his mother would hide a surprise somewhere in his lunch. Sometimes she'd put it in his sandwich; other times, she would stick it inside his apple. And we'd all gather around Larry's desk to see what his mom had given him.

We all had the better lunch pails. We had the comic strips and the action heroes and all that stuff. Nevertheless, we'd all sit around Larry's desk and see what kind of treasure his mom had put into his brown-bag lunch.

Isn't it the same today? We compare our lunch pails with one another. We compare the exterior: who's got the nicer car, who dresses nicer, who's more educated, who has more money, who's got a bigger home, who's got nicer furniture, who's got a nicer body. But the treasure is on the *inside*. It's not what we're doing with our life. We're all trying to figure out what our purpose is through our education, our jobs, our families, our money, and our career advancements. Those things are important too. If you're a doctor, by all means, be the best doctor you can be. But that's not our intended purpose in life. Our intended purpose is to know God and to make Him known.

If you want to know what the purpose of a product is, you have to know what was in the mind of the manufacturer when he made it. If I buy a toaster, take it home, plug it in, and try to get it to give me the local news, I'm going to be disappointed. Why? Because that wasn't in the mind of the manufacturer when he made the toaster.

A toaster was manufactured to toast bread. But if I try and use it for anything else, I'm not going to get the results I want. If I take it back to General Electric and say, "I want my money back; this toaster doesn't work," they're going to plug it in, insert a slice of bread, and tell me, "Sir, it appears to be working just fine." It didn't work for me because I wasn't using it for its intended use.

If I take an automobile and I try to sail to London in it, it's not going to work properly. How come? Because a car is intended to transport people on roads over land, not to be used as a sailboat. If I try to use that car in a different manner than its intended use, it won't work properly. If you want to know the purpose of a product, you have to know what was in the mind of the manufacturer when he made it.

We are all manufactured products. We didn't ask to be born. We didn't ask to be put here. We don't know when we're going to die. We didn't have a decision in the color of our skin, the color of our hair, how tall we were going to be. Why were we manufactured? We have to know what was in the mind of our manufacturer. What was in the mind of God when He manufactured us? What is our purpose in life?

Ultimately, I wasn't created to be a salesman and make money. I'm not saying it's not good to do those things; of course we all have occupations, talents, and careers. Maybe you're a lawyer, and a good one. But your purpose in life isn't to be a lawyer. Your purpose isn't to be a musician, or a writer, or a professional athlete, or a CEO. Your purpose isn't to be whatever you are, whatever you've become, whatever profession you have chosen. That's not our *purpose*.

Our purpose in life, the reason we were manufactured, our intended use is to bring honor to our Creator. That is our purpose. Whatever profession we choose can honor the Creator, but the number one thing we can do to honor our Creator is to accept Jesus Christ for our salvation.

Isn't that the treasure in a brown-bag lunch?

32

GOOD NEWS VERSUS GOOD ADVICE

I don't know who came up with the word "Bible," but I don't like it. I think it can be divisive. I prefer the word "Scriptures," or simply, "God's Word to man." I often call it "God's book of promises," because that's really what it is, the book of promises that God gave to His people.

So there I was, sitting on an airplane, reading God's book of promises, and the guy next to me was reading the paper.

I looked over at him and said, "Can I ask you a question?"

"Sure," he said.

"I'm sitting here reading the Scriptures. How do you feel about that?"

He shrugged.

"Dude, it's none of my business. You do what you want."

"No, no. I get that. I get that I can do what I want. But honestly, when you saw what I was reading, how did it make you feel? I want you to be totally honest with me."

The guy looked at me for a second, probably weighing whether to be totally honest or not.

"You know," he said, "when you pulled out the Scriptures, I thought, 'Man, I wonder if this guy's approachable.'"

I thought that was really interesting.

I asked him what he was reading and he replied, "The New York Times."

"Awesome. What you're reading about in your newspaper is the exact same thing I'm reading about, because in the word of God, it talks about wars, government officials, and businessmen. It talks about people—just like the *New York Times*."

And it's true. The apostle Paul was a tentmaker. He was an amazing businessman. We think of guys like Moses and have all sorts of predefined mental images. We think, *Sure, I know Moses. He led the Israelites out of Egypt, parted the Red Sea, and received the Ten Commandments at Mount Sinai. Case closed.* But did you know Moses grew up in one of the richest economies? That he was one of the best-educated men on the planet? He was also the general of Pharaoh's army. Not too many people know that.

These were business guys and high-ranking government officials. And they were incredible people. The only difference is that in *this* newspaper, it's God's view of what's going on. In the newspapers you and I read today, it's man's view.

The Scriptures are the newspaper I want to read every day. Don't get me wrong; I love reading today's newspapers too. I want to keep up on current events, so I read about what's going on in our government, what's going on in business, and what's happening on Wall Street.

But God's Word brings me news that will really change my life. And there's a big difference between good advice and good news.

Here's an example of good advice. Let's say you lost your job and you're six months behind on your mortgage. You get a phone call from your banker. You know exactly why he's calling.

"I owe you, don't I?" you say.

"Yeah, you're six months behind. But I've got some good advice for you."

"What's that?"

"Well, we have to foreclose on you. Not a big deal. But I have a list of homeless shelters I can give you if you just come by the office. And I found a few people who might be willing to interview you for a job. We did the research for you. You can take your furniture, but you'll need to bring in your key because we're taking the house back in a week."

The advice is great, right? "Here are some homeless shelters! Here are some potential job opportunities! God bless ya." That's all great—but it is most definitely *not* what you need.

Now imagine a very different scenario.

Your banker calls and says, "Hey, it's me, your banker."

"I owe you money, don't I?"

"Yeah, but I've got some good news for you. A guy came by and paid off your mortgage. You own your house now, free and clear. And, oh, by the way, he put $10 million in cash in your bank account and left you the most incredible mansion in Maui. Everything you could ever want has been paid in full for the next fifty years."

Now *that's* good news.

The newspaper may have good advice—stock tips, market data, performance data and analyses—but I want good news. And the good news is that God wants to have a personal relationship with us. I'm going to trust this newspaper—the Scriptures—over the black-and-white newspapers that show up on my front lawn every morning. One of them may help me perform better in the marketplace. The other one can transform not just the way I do business, but also, how I live my life.

Newspapers have news, but Scripture has *really good* news. This is much more than good advice or a crash course in current events. God's book of promises is the kind of good news we can put our hope in. And what is "hope"? Hope is the confident expectation of goodness that will happen in one's life. Just start reading.

Do you believe there is one book that will empower you to "succeed" just by reading and believing it?

33

WHY DON'T YOU ROB A BANK?

Recently, I was asked to come and share some of my experiences with a group of businessmen. So I went in and started talking to these guys.

After a while, one of them said, "You know, Mike, you've been talking a lot about the mercy and grace of God. But it doesn't make sense to me. It feels like you're telling us that we can go do anything we want."

"OK," I replied. "That's not actually what I'm saying, but it does beg another question. We're in a closed group here; nothing goes past that door. So . . . what do you want to do?"

He kind of flinched.

"I don't want to do anything," he said. "But I'm extrapolating from what you're saying that we can do whatever we want because it doesn't matter what we do. We have grace and mercy and forgiveness."

"So what do you want to do?" I asked again. "If you could do anything, anything at all, what would it be?"

"I don't know," he said. "Let's say I wanted to go rob a bank. It sounds to me like you're saying I could go rob a bank because that's going to be forgiven. So why not go rob a bank?"

"Great question," I said. "The real question is, do you want to?"

He started to hem and haw again, but I cut him off.

"I'm just trying to see what you are trying to communicate to me in your heart. Do you want to go rob a bank?"

The man shrugged.

"Well, let's say I did. Yeah, let's say I want to go rob a bank because I wouldn't mind having a million dollars."

"Great," I said. "What's keeping you?"

"God's Word says I'm not supposed to steal."

"Bingo," I said, because we'd finally gotten to the heart of the matter. "Is that really all that's holding you back? So if the book of promises didn't say, 'Thou shalt not steal,' you'd go rob a bank tomorrow? What about the families from which you'd be stealing that money? Or the people in your own life you'd be hurting by committing that act? Are you seeing the bigger picture?"

What this businessman had basically just told me was that he didn't understand grace. Grace makes a person stand back and think, *I don't want to hurt other people like that.* He did not understand what I was saying about mercy and grace—*because he wasn't living under grace.* He was still following a bunch of rules.

That's what I tried to communicate to those businessmen that day, just like I do to all the men and women with whom I speak.

Grace is a game changer.

When we understand the mercy and the grace and the forgiveness of God, it changes us from the inside out. We start thinking and acting differently.

Are you ready to start being a "grace" person and not a "rules" person?

Part VII

GET RICH

♥ | 💰

34

THERE IS GIVING IN RECEIVING

I'm not a pastor, a clergyman, or anything like that. I'm a businessman. And as a businessman, I want to share some principles that God used to change my heart in the area of giving.

I really didn't understand giving until I understood what it meant to receive. Before I accepted that everything I have received is from God, I felt like I had to keep everything for myself.

As businesspeople, we have to go out there and make it happen. You take possession of something and it becomes yours. "I own this. I made this money. I bought this. It's mine. I worked hard. I did the deal. I'm going to take it." And boy, when you have that kind of attitude, it's hard to give. But when I realized that everything I have—my health, my clothes, my car, my home, my income, my friends—is a gift from God, I realized I was receiving from Him. That's when giving became a lot easier.

Let's say you make $1,000 a week, so $52,000 a year. You decide to give $4,000 a year to the Lord's work—half to a missionary organization and half to your church. You're not giving $4,000. You're giving away four weeks of your time.

Let's say, you take $2,000 and give it to a missionary organization so a person can go overseas and spend two weeks in Russia telling people about Jesus Christ. Even though you're staying on American soil, you're doing the same thing as that missionary. You're investing two weeks of your time on the mission field.

That's pretty cool. That means that when you spend two weeks in the office answering phone calls, shuffling paper from the right-hand side of your desk to the left-hand side, typing up proposals—if the money you make during those two weeks goes to people on the mission field, you are also leading people to Jesus Christ. If you're on your mobile phone and you're going from one appointment to the next, conducting business deals and making money over the phone, you're leading people to Christ in your automobile.

Then you take another $2,000 and give it to your church. You've just invested two weeks of time at your church. That money can be used for all manner of things: to pay your pastor, to keep the organization going, to pay the bills, to help fund the church's ministries, to help heal marriages, to lead people to Jesus Christ. People's lives are being changed because of what you gave. You will share in the same reward as the people in these ministries, because you are giving your time in the form of money when you give it away. That is powerful.

If we as businesspeople could realize that the money we give away is our time, that we are doing the work of evangelism by giving, then we'd realize there is giving in receiving.

We're doing that work. Wherever we put our money, that's where we are investing our time and we will share in the same reward. Once we understand that principle, it will change our giving habits.

When I'm working, I know the money I make is being used to further the kingdom of God. I'm in the ministry, and it changes my whole perspective. I want to go to work every day because when I'm making money, I'm helping people.

We don't have to be in "full-time Christian work." We don't have to be ministers or pastors or missionaries. We can be full-time ministers as salespeople, nurses, doctors, lawyers, garbage collectors, lawn-maintenance people, roofers, builders; it doesn't matter. Whatever you do to make money is a form of worship to God when you take that money and give it away.

The money we make for doing our jobs allows us to buy cars and clothes and furniture and nice meals at restaurants and bracelets and watches and earrings. That money is also a gift from God. And when people say, "Wow, you have a nice home," we can say, "Thanks to God. He allowed me to make money to have these nice things. He allowed me to make money to give it away, to help the poor, and to help people who don't have what we have."

Many people in America are wealthy. The problem is, we compare ourselves to each other. We go to Starbucks in our Toyota and see a guy driving a Rolls-Royce. "Man, that guy is wealthy," we say.

Try this on for size: When you start comparing yourself to the rest of the world, you *are* wealthy. A person is in the top 1 percent of the world's population if his or her income is $2,000 a month. If that describes you, then you are abundantly wealthy compared to the people of India and China and Cuba and the Third World countries who are making less than a dollar a day. So let's stop comparing ourselves to those in our immediate worlds, our bosses and VPs and C-suite executives. If we're going to make a comparison, then let's compare ourselves to the world. God has blessed us richly. Our wealth is a blessing from His hand.

Say you go up to your best friend, the person you trust the most, and say, "Will you loan me a penny?"

It's silly because the amount is so small. It might be hard for you to ask for a million dollars, but a penny is no big deal.

Let me tell you something. What you have today is a penny in the eyes of God. You may be worth millions and have more assets than anyone you know, but it's still just a penny in the eyes of the Creator.

How wealthy is God? Before anything existed, before there was a world, a sun, a universe, a solar system, a galaxy, before there was anything, there was God. And in Himself, He was rich. In Himself, everything existed. Everything was in Him before He spoke it into existence.

Your wealth is a penny, but every penny makes a difference in the lives of others. "Take a penny; leave a penny," as the saying goes. What you have been given by God is now yours to give.

Do you have a penny?

35

THE TRINITY OF GIVING

I looked up the word "black" in the dictionary. Here's the definition: "dark."

I looked up "dark." Definition: "obscure."

I looked up "obscure." Definition: "faded."

I looked up "faded." Definition: "pale."

I looked up "pale." Definition: "off-white."

I looked up "off-white." Definition: "a shade of white."

Isn't that something? You start with "black" and end up with "white." It doesn't make sense to me.

But here's the deal: life doesn't always make sense. We don't "get it" all the time. This is the perspective I need to take into the marketplace, because it's exactly what I must do. I need to transform my way of thinking.

What does that mean when I'm in the marketplace? What do I do? How do I walk that out?

First, before we can walk anything out, we have to embrace it to the point that we truly believe it. Not a mental assent, but a belief in our core: "I actually believe this so it will change my life." And for me, when I'm with people, that means giving. I like to give of myself because God gives and gives and gives to me.

Giving is one of the key areas of a businessman's life in which he can actually change the world around himself. And there are three main ways to give.

Number one: **Give compliments.** Giving compliments is super fun. That's the first thing we can do for people: find a way to compliment and encourage them. People never forget a compliment. Do you ride an elevator on the way to work? Great. Find a way to talk to someone, to compliment a colleague on her hair or her scarf or her smile. Tell that guy from accounting how much you love his briefcase or his cheerful spirit. Find a way to compliment people for something because they won't forget it; it gives them a boost and brightens their day.

Number two: **Give gifts.** Give gifts to people. Now, I'm not talking about going out and buying a $1,000 gift. I'm talking about something really small. Notice people. Next time you go into your colleague's office, take note that she has twenty pens on her desk. Then if you're at the store and see a cute pen, you might remember your colleague and buy it for her. "You know,

I saw you like pens. I thought you might want to try this."
"How thoughtful!" she'll say, and be totally touched.
People love to feel special, and little gifts make them
feel that way, even if it's just a cup of coffee. Bring a gift
to someone. These are simple things anybody can do.

Number three: **Give your time.** This is maybe the
most vague—and it can also be the hardest to do.
We're all so stressed and time-crunched that we can
be pretty protective of our time. We feel like we can't
afford to spare even one second because our days are
scheduled down to the minute.

That makes it all the more powerful when you give
someone your time. Carve out time for a coffee date
with someone, or lunch, or even just five minutes to
sit across from a friend and let her tell you about her
day, listening without judgment (and no looking at
your watch). That's a huge gift. This is the stuff people
remember.

These are the three ways we can give. We can give
compliments, we can give gifts, and we can give our
time. Try to find subtle ways to implement these three
forms of giving in the marketplace with other people—
not only with your families, but everywhere you go.

I try to give compliments every day. Just the other
morning, I was at my neighborhood grocery store,
and I said to the checker, "Ma'am, I just want to let
you know: I've seen you at this checkout counter for

months, and your attitude is so fantastic. You always smile. I've never seen you get impatient or frustrated. Maybe you're told to do that by your employer—to always smile—but you know what? You don't have to and you do so anyway. I think that's genuine and I just want you to know I noticed."

And then I walked away.

What, then, happens to that woman? Who knows what's going on with her? She may be having a great day, or she may be on the brink of suicide. There's no way we can know that, of course, but that's the point: we don't know how our words support and encourage people. Those same words change not only their recipient but also, us. Giving a compliment takes me out of myself, as I get to help others.

Once I change my view so that I'm looking outside myself, I see increasing opportunities to give people gifts. Something I can hand to them that will make them go, "Wow, this is really cool," or a kind word or a gift of time. I drive by a guy on the side of the road who is changing a tire, and I stop and help him. I see an older lady struggling to get her cart out of the mall, and I say, "Ma'am, can I help you with that?" That takes a few minutes of my time, yes. But it's a revolutionary way to live in the world. This is the first step we can use to change the environments in our market space—and we don't see a lot of it today.

You also want to be honest with yourself about your intention in giving gifts. A lot of people may ask, "If I give compliments or little gifts, or if I donate some of my time, what am I going to get back?" They use gift giving as a manipulative technique. I understand that, but that's not what I'm talking about.

To be able to give selflessly helps you more than it helps others, because you're not expecting anything in return. And when that happens, the things that will come your way will be much greater than what you think you could have received through manipulative giving.

The key to genuine gift giving is simple: give when you do not need (or expect) anything in return. It's the attitude of, "I'm giving because I want to give." God sees that.

If you make God's business your business, God will make your business His business. And if God makes your business His business . . . wow!

What does it mean to make God your business?

Develop the generous habits I'm recommending. I'm not saying you have to give half your income. I'm talking about the giving of yourself. You have something to teach me. I want to learn from you. That's humility, remember? We must humble ourselves enough to learn from others. And then reach out and give.

Now at times, are you going to go, "Man, if I do this, I know I can get something in return"? Sure—we're human. But that's not the purpose. The purpose is to selflessly give, not expecting anything in return, because then the One who owns all things can give us things we never dreamed we could receive.

What are you dreaming for that only God can give?

36

THE SEEN AND THE UNSEEN

People often come up to me after an event and ask what I did to get to where I am. These people tend to be young and ambitious. "How do you do it, Mike?" they ask, hoping I'll deliver the magic mantra or buzzword that will propel them into unprecedented success. "How'd you get to the top?"

What I tell them is: "Pay attention to the seen *and* unseen."

The "seen" is the stuff you can easily articulate, the problems of which you're fully aware. Let's take our man Tony, a great guy who's the number-one sales rep at his company. Tony gets to the office by 8:30 a.m. every morning and does exactly what he's supposed to do. He's very attentive to his clients, and when he receives an email message from one of them, he always makes sure to respond within five minutes. Tony has a disciplined, regimented day in the office, and he makes sure that, three days a week, he spends off-campus hours with his clients. It's easy to get a client to go to lunch because they've all got to eat, but to get them to choose to meet up after hours when they could be home with their family—that means Tony has to develop a deeper relationship with them. So he's making sure all those things are happening.

Tony's also getting deals right and pricing properly. He's doing all the right things to be a great salesman. He remembers to ask one client about her daughter's sixth birthday and another client about his son graduating from college. But then, a lot of other salespeople do these same things. These actions and behaviors on their own aren't responsible for Tony's rise to the top.

That's where the "unseen" come in. These are the things you can't necessarily see that set Tony apart.

For the last thirty years, Tony has been giving a minimum of 20 percent of his gross annual income to the poor. He feels that the business community has to fund the kingdom of God, because without God, there would be no business community. And, the way Tony sees it, there would be no missionaries and no churches without the business community. His heart is eager as a businessman to help support God's work, because he knows any intrinsic skills he has as a salesman are a gift from God.

That's what people don't see. They don't see the fact that every morning before he comes to work, Tony prays, "Lord, I am your son. I'm not a servant. And as your son, I'm asking you for people to see that there's a man of God on planet Earth in business who follows you and believes in you and talks about you." That's the unseen part of what makes Tony a success.

Also unseen is all the work Tony does to stay connected both to God and to other people. It becomes much more than a job; it becomes a lifestyle. When people ask Tony how many hours a week he works, he says, "168 hours a week."

"You're a workaholic!" they cry.

"Ask me how many hours I play," he says.

"Fine, how many hours do you play?"

"168."

When they scratch their head in confusion, Tony grins.

"For me, there's not a division between work and play. I'm just living my life. Business and pleasure are the same, or why do it? Maybe Tony is a master in the art of living!"

We all want to compartmentalize. "God first, family second, job third, ourselves last." You know what? These old adages don't fit anymore. Crack that thinking open, because you can't compartmentalize a human life. Tony works *and* plays all day long. That's the unseen secret that has helped him rise to the top—and the same can be true for you.

How do you divide your days? Do you dread the time you spend at work and count the hours until you can go back home? Who wants to live a life like that?! That sounds awful to me.

Maybe, if the "seen" parts of your life aren't working for you, it's time to devote some attention to the "unseen." Maybe you carve out ten minutes to pray every morning, or ten minutes in the evening to read Scripture. Maybe you think about giving or finding an organization you really want to support. If you go back to your private world, the world of just you and God, you'll be amazed by how the "seen" aspects of who you are will begin to transform.

Can you articulate the unseen parts of your life that have made you who you are today?

37

GIVING FROM WITHIN

Have you ever heard anyone say the following? "Christians are the last people on Earth with whom I'd want to do business. You can't trust them."

We've got to get rid of that perception!

We have to share the truth about the God of the universe, not the version in which I call myself a Christian and keep cheating, stealing, and taking advantage. We have to look at God in the way He wants us to see Him. We have to see ourselves the way He sees us, and furthermore, see each other the way He sees other people.

When you sit down with somebody to make a deal, you may not agree with what the other person believes, but you are still going to show her respect. You are going to shower her with respect, love, and integrity. You're going to be upfront and honest with her. Of course you don't want to lose! I love that. But if you can walk out the truth of what you believe, it's going to set you apart from all those so-called Christians who use God to cheat and lie and steal.

If you just got married, how difficult would it be for you to present a dozen roses to your spouse on your honeymoon? Not hard at all, right? You wouldn't have to think twice about it, because you're moved from within.

What has to happen to us as businessmen and women in the marketplace—or alone, in our private worlds—is that we move differently *from the inside*. We're not under any obligation; we don't have to do anything, but we want to.

You don't have to go to church on Sunday. You *get* to. You *get* to be around people. You don't have to *do* anything. That's old religion. That's the old paradigm that has to be crushed inside of our hearts. We don't have to do anything once we know Christ.

We finally *get* to receive. And when I become a receiving receptacle, all I can do is give it away to other people. That's the God we get to demonstrate in the marketplace. When other people see that, they begin to change.

I'm not talking about the old system. "You can't do business with him, boy. You'd better be careful. Hold your wallet. Hold your purse. Hold your kids." Let's kill that once and for all. Let's stop thinking that way.

We get a choice. I get to choose what to believe. That's true freedom. I get to choose to change the belief system that has held me captive my whole life. How do I do that? By believing the book of promises. My family changes, my kids change, the world around me changes, and the marketplace changes—all because *I* change. The ripple effect is huge.

My question to us is this: What do we have to do to get rid of that old paradigm? To free the real person trapped inside us? How do we dig out that little boy or girl, the innocent child in us who wants to come out and play and believe what our Creator says?

Our goal is to bring that wonderful child to the playground, which is the marketplace today.

Part VIII

CHANGED

♥ | 💰

38

LET YOUR CLUBS DO THE TALKING

There's a young guy in pro golf who has been making quite a name for himself recently. And it's not exactly the name you want.

This kid is only twenty-four years old. In one year, he captured three PGA Tour titles and became the youngest winner of a World Golf Championship. Not too shabby.

But when he was interviewed after the win, he said, "I have [had] three wins out here on the PGA Tour. I just don't see a lot of guys that have done that, besides Tiger Woods, of course, and, you know, the other legends of the game. It's just one of those things, I believe in myself and—especially with how hard I've worked—I'm one of the top five players in the world."

His comment blew up on social media, with people accusing him of being cocky, arrogant, and even downright delusional. No one doubts that the kid has talent, but he got hammered for drawing that kind of attention to himself. "Who do you think you are?" people demanded. "Just because you made the FedExCup standings' top five doesn't mean you're one of the top five golfers in the world."

Proverbs 27:2 says, "Let another praise you, and not your own mouth; a stranger, and not your own lips." Solomon said that—the wisest guy on the planet. In fact, the Scripture says that not only was Solomon the wisest man on Earth back then; he was also the wisest man ever to live.

It's always better to have praise come from someone else's mouth. It's why, when you're speaking in front of a big group, it's customary for someone else to give the introduction. Otherwise, you're up there going, "Hey, everybody, I've spoken in twenty countries and won ten awards. They say I'm the best speaker on the planet. There's nobody as good as I am. And so, with that, let me begin my talk." If I began a presentation that way, you'd better believe the room would be half empty by the time I got to my first point!

But if someone else comes out and gives me a glowing introduction, and then I come onstage and humbly begin my talk, I'm going to get a very different reaction from the crowd. Arrogance is a repellent, but humility is a huge attractor.

In my field of sales, you could say I've achieved a lot. I've gotten the awards, the trips—all that stuff. But I don't see that as some masterful success of my own doing. I feel God gave me the talents to be a good salesman. That's where my passion is, and I'm good at doing what I do. But if I want to draw people closer to my heart, I don't tell them how great I am. I don't put confidence in myself, because that's arrogance. Instead, I put confidence in the gift I was given. That's humility.

If you're gifted, you should absolutely put confidence into your gift. I put confidence into my ability to sell. The power of persuasion is a gift. God puts me in situations where I can exercise that gift and use it to bless the world in which we live. But when the gift gets confused with "Who I Am," and I claim it as part of my identity, then it gets warped into arrogance. And if anyone questions my gift, I get angry, because I've started to think the gift is rightly mine.

We all have jobs, which means we all have functions. Your function can either define you, or you can use it as the gift God gave you. You can take that lesson into any CEO's office in the world—IBM, Apple, Facebook—and it still holds true. The moment you say, "I made it so far, and now I'm the best, and this defines me as a human being," you've just thrown away the gift.

A job cannot define you as a human being. It's impossible. Just like golf cannot define you. Your wife can't define you. Your kids can't define you. Your hobbies can't define you. What you *can* do is take the gifts you have—being able to play golf, being good at sales, creating a Fortune 500 company, whatever—and use them to let the world see how God is working through you.

The word "define" actually means to limit. So when you're defining yourself in terms of some attribute, whether it's your marriage or your golf swing, you're not making yourself greater. You're actually limiting yourself because you're describing yourself in very one-dimensional terms.

There's a kind of accepted ethos in golf that, when you win, you should be humble about it. Let your clubs do the talking.

Very few people know this, but at the eighteenth hole in the last Masters he played in, Gary Player got on his knees and kissed the green and thanked God for allowing him to borrow this gift.

How cool is that? "Thank you for allowing me to borrow this gift." Not, "I'm one of the best players in the world. I'm amazing. My talent is off the charts." But, "This talent was never mine to begin with. You've let me borrow it for a while, God, so, thanks."

We'd all do well to treat our talents and abilities as "gifts," and let our clubs do the talking. Won't the rest take care of itself?

39

BE A UFC FIGHTER

Who says we can't have humility and also be fierce competitors in the marketplace? The two aren't mutually exclusive, though we often act like they are.

Humility does not mean weakness. It actually means strength. If you're humble, you are able to give credit where credit is due, whether to a colleague, a boss, an employee, or—yes—even a competitor. But in no way does that mean you have to go belly-up and keep your competitive impulses at bay.

It's important for us as businesspeople to take this message and not be ashamed of it. Be the toughest competitors on the planet. Treat your business like the Ultimate Fighting Championship, and be a UFC fighter every day you go to work. There's nothing wrong with that!

There was a UFC heavyweight champion that I loved to watch. He wouldn't lose. He just wouldn't. I'd see this guy fight, and I'd be thinking, *Are you kidding me?!* He was unreal.

And what did he say after a fight? "I just want to thank Jesus."

Now that's humility. Here's a guy who is as tough as nails on the outside—but he's strong internally too. He's a competitor. He's not going to lose. And then when the fight is over, he gives credit where credit is due: to God.

Why can't we all be that way? Though it's probably too late for us to be real UFC fighters, we *can* bring that fighting spirit to the marketplace every single time we do business. We can be fierce, and we can be humble.

Businesspeople who embrace humility are true fighters because when they win, they win with humility, and when they lose, they lose with humility.

You're not going to get every deal or close every sale. But I'll tell you one thing: if you carry humility out into the marketplace, if you bring that spirit with you to every transaction, you will reap the rewards.

Whether you win or lose, you'll be fighting the UFC way.

40

KEEP THE DREAM ALIVE

I recently spoke at a university in Macedonia, and I'm not sure I've ever enjoyed such an eager, optimistic audience. The auditorium was full of hundreds of college students soaking up every word that came out of my mouth.

"How do we do this?" they wanted to know. "How do we get to where we want to be?"

"Tell me," I said. "What do you guys dream about?"

One twenty-year-old guy stood up and said, "I want to be an actor in Hollywood."

You know what was interesting? Nobody laughed. Put that same kid in a roomful of jaded cynics in Los Angeles, California, and you'll get a whole lot of eye rolls. *Everybody* in Los Angeles wants to be an actor in Hollywood or knows somebody who does.

So I asked this young man, "Do you really believe that?"

And he said, "Yeah."

"Great," I said. "I love that dream. What are you doing to get yourself there?"

"I'm taking acting lessons."

"Awesome. What else?"

He looked a little sheepish.

"I'm not sure what else to do."

I had an idea for him.

"Social media is huge. Why don't you put something on YouTube: a monologue or a sketch? Just go for it. Do you know how much stuff goes viral that nobody thought would go viral? There are dozens of models and actors who were 'discovered' on YouTube. You have to start putting yourself out there."

He nodded and grinned at me.

I looked at all those earnest young men and women and said, "Do not give up on your dream. You don't know where that dream will lead you." I pointed to the brave young man who had stood up. "Look at my friend here. Maybe his passion for acting will lead him to be a director or a producer. Maybe he'll end up acting in commercials or starring in a Broadway play. The point is: God may lead you in a totally different direction, but it's the dream that will get you there."

Shortly after I got back from Macedonia, I spoke at a prominent company in the States. The audience was composed of 250 people, the vast majority of them, between the ages of forty and sixty. Compared to the hope and optimism of the college students in Macedonia, these men and women were at the polar-opposite end of the spectrum. They were disillusioned, disheartened, and depressed.

"The economy shattered our dreams," they said. "The government pressed us down. We can't do anything."

This time the person who stood up was the guy in charge of human resources, a man everybody in the company looked up to. Only he didn't stand up; he just sat there and heckled me. Everything I said or suggested, he'd respond, "Yeah, we can't do that." "We tried that, but it didn't work." "Nope, won't work. Not here."

Finally, I said, "You know what? I want you to stand up for a minute and come on up to the front."

He shrugged and strode to the front of the room. You could tell the kind of person he was just by the way he walked: the egotistical genius, the guy who thinks he knows everything.

Once he was standing beside me, I turned to the crowd of 250 people.

"Is this guy a leader?" I asked.

People nodded.

"Yes!"

"Do you listen to what he says?"

"Yes."

I turned back to face him.

"You're a leader because people listen to what you say. So what if you changed your talk track? What if you were encouraging instead of discouraging? What if you said, 'We can do something. We can make a change'?"

He shifted his weight to his other leg. I could tell he didn't like where this was going.

"I imagine it's pretty boring for you," I said, "to get your paycheck every week and go home to be miserable. Your wife must pick up on it, and so do your children. Your kids want to grow up to be just like Dad—but Dad is miserable.

"So what would it feel like if you did the opposite? What if you were a motivational speaker instead of a naysayer? Because you've got it inside you; I can tell. You're vocal, you're a confident guy, and you're not afraid to tell me what's going on. So now I want you to tell me how to fix it. You tell me, OK? I want you to take over here."

With that, I went and sat in the front row.

"Keep it positive," I coached.

This same guy who'd been so cocksure a few minutes earlier suddenly looked flustered.

"Well, uh, if we . . ."

"No!" I cut him off. "No ifs. That's wrong. 'If' is the wrong word. Keep going."

Slowly, he became more comfortable. He talked for fifteen minutes—and wouldn't you know it, he started saying positive stuff. He started telling his colleagues what they *could* do, instead of focusing on what they couldn't. And you could see people's eyes light up. They wanted to be a part of something positive. They dreamed about being part of something big.

When do we lose our dreams? Why do we give them up? Younger people still have them, but as we age, we toss our dreams aside for the "reality" (whatever that means) of our daily lives.

I don't care if you're forty and divorced and disillusioned with all life has to offer. I don't care if you're seventy-two and feel like life has used you up. I don't care if you've just lost your job and are back in your parents' basement, wondering what God has in store for you. You know the one thing every success story has in common? It's about someone who never gave up. That person kept the dream alive, even through the greatest adversity.

When do you give up? When you die! That's the only acceptable reason to stop trying!

41

MARGIN

I travel a lot for business, and I used to be very bad at it. In the past, if I was leaving on a Thursday afternoon and traveling from Dallas to Frankfurt, I would say, "I can go out for dinner on Wednesday night. I don't leave till Thursday at four o'clock, so I can probably squeeze in a meeting that morning, pack at noon, and still make my flight."

Guess what? If one thing was off, even by an hour, it screwed everything up. If my meeting that morning ran long, I missed my flight. If I packed poorly and had to run back to the house for something I'd forgotten, I missed my flight. And it wasn't always stuff I was in control of. Once I was coming back from Frankfurt for a dinner with important clients. My flight was supposed to land at three o'clock Monday afternoon. Well, the flight got delayed, and I missed the client dinner—and the sale.

Around that time I read a book called *Margin* by Richard A. Swenson, MD. It was a real life-changer for me. Margin is one of the most important things we, as businesspeople, have an opportunity to implement in our own lives—meaning, if I'm leaving Thursday on a four o'clock flight, I don't do anything the night before. I stay at home with my family and we cook a steak, open a nice bottle of wine, and relax. I pack a little bit, then come back out to the grill and make sure the steaks aren't burning. Then I go back in and put some socks in my bag. I take my time. I need that margin because I don't know what's going to happen.

The next morning, I do tasks but I don't push things. I make sure I have margin on the front end and the back end. Now when I travel, I make sure I return home on a Friday, not on a Monday, when I have to go to work right away. I need the weekend to wind down, recoup, and make use of that margin time. I get back into my private world and think, *OK, what do I need to be doing for myself? What do I need to be doing for my family?* I take that private time before I jump back into my public, professional life.

Not many of us take that time. We cram so many things into our lives that we often miss relationships.

When I talk about bringing relationships back into business, that's what I'm talking about. The more margin we have, the more we are able to give more generously and think more clearly when we're at work.

You won't get margin unless you plan for it. It's part of being prepared. That's one thing I love about what former mayor Rudy Giuliani did in New York City prior to 9–11–2001. He prepared. He planned. He would sit down and meet on a monthly basis with the department heads and leaders of city agencies (police, fire, emergency services, etc.). They met to determine what would happen if a disaster occurred in the city. They planned what they would need to do to ensure strong communications within the city, to respond well if disaster struck.

Compare this with what happened in the wake of Hurricane Katrina in New Orleans four years later. Disaster struck, and the city was unprepared. One mayor prepared, and the disaster put the spotlight on the planning. The other mayor didn't plan, and the disaster put the spotlight on the lack of planning.

Giuliani understood margin.

We can all do the same thing. We need margin to talk to our Father. He made us. People didn't make us. Our boss didn't make us. *God* made us. So we need time alone with Him.

Jesus had margin. He reflected. He went out into the wilderness to be alone. He spent time with His Father to do the great things He had to do. He took that time for His private life, before going back out into the public with His disciples and the people He loved.

Your margin will probably look different from my margin. The morning is a sacred time for me. People know not to call me in the morning, because I'm not available. Now, if it's an emergency, that's a different story. But if you just want to chat, you're going to have to wait, because I need that margin time in the morning to set my day, my heart, and my mind. My morning is when I map out the day and plan what I'm going to do. That way, the rest of the day I can be happy, grounded, and available to the people in my world.

What margin can you build into your life?

42

PREPARE FOR IMPACT

What kind of impact do you have on the people around you?

As a businessperson, you interact with others every day, even if you're an independent contractor or a freelancer who works from home. We live in such an interconnected world today that we'd be fools to think we *don't* leave an impact on the people with whom we come in contact. Of course we do.

Here are some questions to ask yourself every time you interact with another human being: *How can I help this person see how much value she has? How can I help her see the importance of the impact she has on the world? And how can I help this person make even more of an impact?*

I like to think of myself as an impactor. When I can actually help someone make more of an impact—when

I can help pull it out of him or her—it fuels me. It's not about me anymore. My value in life is catalyzed when I find the value in someone else.

Perhaps you have heard the old adage, "If you assume something is true about another person, you will look for that thing. When you look for it, you will find it. And when you find it, you will respond to it." It all starts with an assumption. And if our assumptions are wrong, then our response is apt to be wrong too.

If you assume your boss is a heartless jerk, you're going to find him to be a horrible person. If you assume your coworkers are incompetent cretins, you're going to find them to be absolutely intolerable. If you assume your wife is a bickering nag, you're going to find her nagging at every turn. So if it's true our assumptions are self-fulfilling prophecies, why do we waste time assuming negative things about the people in our lives?

We all assume because it's human nature. But here's the good news: it works in the opposite direction too. If I assume you are a valuable, impactful, influential human—no matter what you do or accomplish—then I'm going to look for that value inside you. And when I find it, I'll show it to you.

What am I looking for in people? Value. Integrity. Talent. Strength. Passion. And why am I looking for these things? So that I can help people find the value, integrity, talent, strength, and passion within themselves.

Once they've found it, they can watch these attributes transform their lives. That's the sort of philosophy we have to walk out in business. Make "Prepare for impact!" your motto—and not just your own impact, but also the impact of the other people in your life.

Unfortunately, not everyone in business walks this out. So often you go sit down in a room with three blue suits, and these guys are comparing briefcase sizes, how much money they have, who drives a nicer car, and their fancy C-suite titles. They make it abundantly clear that they don't want to have a meeting with a bunch of grunts; they're too high up on the totem pole for that. Everything in their demeanor says they don't want to be there.

But what if they took a different approach? What if one of the top guys in your company walked in and said, "Hi. I run this organization; I'm the top dog. But today, I want to sit down with you guys and really *see* you. At the end of the day, you guys are making this company successful. Without you, I don't know where I'd be; you all make such a huge impact on this organization every day. So I want to know: What do *you* think? What do you think we should be doing?"

I want to see leaders influence their teams like that. What a different corporate culture that would be!

Can you imagine?

43

THE LIARS' CLUB

Look me in the eye and tell me you've never lied.
Not once in your life. Not ever, not to anyone.

If you tell me that, I'll *know* you're a liar.

We've all lied, haven't we? Little white lies, good-natured fibs, maybe even some gigantic whoppers. You've done it at least once, probably a lot more often than once. You've lied to your parents or your kids, your boss or your coworkers. Maybe your partner gained a little weight and asked, "How do I look in this outfit?"— and you lied to protect her feelings. Whatever your rationale was, at some point in your life, you've lied.

The real trouble comes when we lie to "get ahead"— to advance in our careers or to pretend to be something we're not. My friend Bob experienced this firsthand. Bob was the president of a company. When he was ready to retire, he looked at the three vice presidents below him, Joe, Don, and Vivian, and wanted to determine who was fit to take the reins.

So, Bob gave each one of them a packet of seeds and he said, "I want you to go home and plant these seeds. And in two months, you're going to come back and everybody will present his or her plants to the group. Based on your results, I'll make a decision about who will be the next president."

So they all went home and got their pots and put the soil in and planted their seeds. A couple of weeks went by, and they started talking to each other about how it was going.

Joe said to Don, "Hey, dude, what about your plant? What's going on?"

"I think mine's a vegetable. I can tell, man. I mean, you know, it's starting to grow. It's about four inches and it's green. How about you?"

"I don't know, man. I think it could be a fruit. Or a flower. It's too early to say," Joe said.

They turned to Vivian.

"I've got nothing. I can't get anything to grow," Vivian said. The two men looked at her with pity.

A couple months went by and Joe and Don were still bragging about their plants. Vivian still had nothing.

She went home and said to her husband, "Honey, I'm in trouble. What did I do wrong? I killed it. I mean, there's nothing growing. I've got to bring back a pot with a live plant inside. This is embarrassing. I'm a vice president. I'm in line to be the next in charge."

So the day came. They all brought in their plants. Joe had a little pink flower. Don had a tomato vine. And Vivian had an empty pot. Bob walked in and examined all the pots.

"OK, guys. Congratulate your new president."

They looked at each other, not sure whom to congratulate.

"Well, which one of us is it?" Don asked.

"The one who didn't grow anything," Bob told them.

Joe and Don both looked annoyed. Don turned beet red, and Joe folded his arms over his chest.

"How come you chose her?" Joe huffed.

"Because all the seeds I gave you were dead. And I wanted to see who had the integrity to come in here with an empty pot."

Instead of being honest about their impotent plants, Joe and Don had manipulated the process. What if they had been honest like Vivian had been? Then Bob would have had a harder decision to make. As it stood, there was no question: Vivian became president of the company.

Lying doesn't make you bad or evil; it makes you human. But choosing integrity and honesty over lies? That makes you a human after God's own heart.

Speaking of God's heart, who knows it? Is it demanding? Angry? Jealous? Is God disappointed by the choices you've made in life? Is He frustrated with where you "ended" up? Did you "screw up" the plans He had for you? Are you in *His* will, or completely out of it?

Simply put, what does it mean to be a "person after God's heart"?

Without getting into stories of history written for our edification in the Scriptures, one man actually was called "a man after God's own heart": David, the one who became King of Israel. The factual information about his life is as accurate, if not more accurate, than any other piece of history ever written on planet Earth.

Why was David called "a man after God's own heart"? What did he do to attain such a unique title? This is the only time in Scripture that God defines one of his creations this way. The answer is pretty straight-forward: because David knew, experienced, saw, and lived God's forgiveness. He knew that God is faithful when we are not. God is forgiving when we are not. God shows mercy when we don't.

David knew all that. He witnessed it firsthand, because, boy, oh boy, did David screw up. He made a royal mess of things! He committed adultery. He ordered a man killed. And yet he knew that God did not deal with him on the basis of his behavior, nor punish him according to his mistakes. Now *that* is an understanding and forgiving God.

I heard a man say once that revival occurs when God gets tired of man misrepresenting Him, so He shows up and performs miracles and healings to those who don't deserve it—at least not in our eyes. Why does He do it? To protect *His* own good name.

Now that's a God I can get excited about! That's a God I can boldly talk about, not some religious-mumbo-jumbo authoritarian God, or some rules-and-regulations advisor in the sky.

The God of David is a *real* God, active in a real marketplace, with real people as they make real mistakes, talking about real things—and not hiding their real fears.

Are you ready to get rid of the lies and start telling the truth about God, about Scripture, and about who you really are?

Final Thoughts

GET OFF THE NAIL!

Here is one story that pretty much summarizes everything I've been trying to tell you throughout this book

Bob is a pretty normal guy. Every morning he wakes up and gets ready to go to his job as a janitor at a middle school forty-five minutes away. He barely sees his kids in the mornings since they're getting ready for school. Most days, he manages to give his wife a quick kiss as she is getting ready for her job as a middle manager at an office downtown. He downs some juice and some bacon, gets in his car, and drives the forty-five minutes to work, where he spends most of his day scraping off gum and cleaning up vomit. Bob works an eight-hour shift, not including his lunch break, and feels pretty pummeled by the end of the day.

After nine hours, he gets back in his car and fights the traffic home. At night, he likes to spend at least a little time with his kids, who have had completely different days than he has, and he tries to stay focused on what's going on in their lives. He also wants to attend to his bride to hear about her day and make sure she's doing all right. Bob has had a very long day, but he knows it's important to make time for these important relationships. They have dinner together as a family, Bob washes the dishes, and together they watch a couple hours of TV. Afterward, he and his wife talk in bed for maybe five minutes before they both fall asleep, exhausted.

Bob is a decent guy, but he isn't exactly moving forward. Sure, he'd love to have a better, more exciting relationship with God. He'd even love to implement some big changes in his life. But what does that look like? How does Bob push himself out of the daily grind to have a life that's exciting and fun and purposeful?

It doesn't actually take a lot for us to radically change our lives. Sometimes it starts with simply sitting down and taking an assessment. Where can you add what to your life? There are a million small, practical things you might do differently.

For example, Bob has a forty-five-minute drive to and from work each day. What is he listening to on that drive? Most days, he doesn't think much about it. He usually just turns on the radio and listens to whatever is on, whether it's a bunch of garbage music or a radio talk show that subjects him to the DJ's opinions on politics for forty minutes. (Who is that guy, anyway, and why does anyone care what he thinks?)

Bob may not be in control of the rest of his day, but he has complete control over those ninety minutes. Maybe he could start listening to motivating topics that encourage him to follow his dreams. Or he could listen to Scripture to find out what *God* thinks, an opinion that carries a lot more weight than some random radio DJ. Bob usually begrudges the many hours he spends each week stuck in bumper-to-bumper traffic, but he's actually been given a great opportunity. He has been given this precious sliver of time to learn, think, and grow. It's never too late to keep learning, to find and cultivate new passions—especially if they could potentially change his life.

But, as we all know, change is hard, and most of us don't want to do it. Take the following parable: Two guys are sitting on a porch, each enjoying a strong cup of coffee. One guy has a dog, and the dog is lying at his feet, howling.

It doesn't seem to bother the man at all, the dog's howling, but his friend is going nuts.

"Your dog has been howling for the last half hour," he says. "What's bothering him?"

The man shrugs.

"He's howling because he's sitting on a nail."

"He's sitting on a nail?!"

"Yep."

The guy without the dog is baffled.

"Then why doesn't he get off the nail?"

"Oh," says the man with the dog. "I guess because he doesn't find it painful enough yet. For all he knows, if he got off the nail, it might hurt even worse!"

Isn't that a great parable for our lives? We perceive the pain of staying where we're at to be less than the pain of changing. It's why many people have trouble leaving abusive relationships or getting sober when they struggle with addiction. They may be in a great deal of pain, but it's still scarier to change their situation, because they don't know what lies in wait on the other side.

But once that pain hits a certain level, most people say, "I'm done. I can't do this anymore." That's when the dog finally gets up off the nail and stops howling—and when people finally make the changes they need to make in their lives.

Bob isn't miserable, but he's not exactly happy, either. The nail in his life isn't excruciating—at least, not yet. He's not satisfied or fulfilled, and he's never thrilled to get out of bed in the morning and start another long day. Right now, he's stuck in a strange kind of limbo, a comfort zone that feels a little too dull to be satisfying, but a little too comfortable to make a change.

So many of us are afraid to try something new. We get in these comfort zones, which sounds harmless enough. What we forget is: some of these comfort zones are really destructive. Instead of pushing ourselves to learn a new skill or practice, we come home and spend four hours a night watching TV. How can God live through us in our talents while we're watching television?

There is nothing that kills our souls faster than lingering in our comfort zones. We have to get out of them. We have to get off the nail.

I'm not saying that there's no pain when we do that. Of course there is! When we're out of our comfort zone, that pain absolutely comes flowing in—and that's when the greatest changes occur in our lives.

Change requires challenging our belief system. And challenging our belief system is very uncomfortable.

Will you dare to believe what is most uncomfortable to you?

Afterword

Let me leave you with one final thought and some questions to consider and perhaps discuss with your friends and family.

Most people have had previous expectations about where they would be in business or their personal life. And they realize that those expectations they'd had for their life are nowhere near their present reality. There is a huge gap in between.

I am not talking about expectations that are impossible to achieve. If I expected to try out for the NBA and be accepted by the Boston Celtics, chances are pretty close to impossible that would ever become a reality.

But even our more realistic expectations don't always match our real lives. Just consider your expectations for where you thought you would be in business financially or professionally, and compare that to your present reality.

Is it wrong to have expectations? No, but "expectations" might not be the most helpful word to use.

Unmet expectations usually produce a sense of "What is wrong with me?" or "I'm not good enough." That gap is where we fall into feelings of despair, loneliness, self-condemnation, sadness, hopelessness, or blame. The list is endless when we lose hope that we will ever be what we thought or expected we would be.

I believe a more appropriate word would be "goals." Goals are achievable. Learning to properly set goals is key for anyone in business—or in life, for that matter.

Consider the story of John R. Noe, author of *High Performance: Principles for High Achievers*. In his book, he describes not being able to open the drawer to his desk because his belly was in the way. That motivated him to change. He decided that he was going to climb the Matterhorn, a mountain in the Alps that straddles the border between Switzerland and Italy. The Matterhorn is considered one of the top ten hardest mountains to climb in the world, according to Rough Guides.

What if he had expected to do this the next day? That gap between reality and expectation would cause feelings of despair, and he might have done nothing. But instead, he learned to set goals. He started with walking around the block once a day. Then he was walking around twice, then running, then enrolling himself and his family in climbing/repelling school. You get the idea: small goals to eventually reach his dream.

And a couple years later, Mr. Noe was sitting on top of the Matterhorn!

Bottom line, when we replace our expectations with goals, we are motivated by the journey, not driven by the result. Even if we never reach our desired end result, we are much further along, and the process has become our way of life.

So, enjoy the following questions and take time to ponder them. As you do, you may find that what you believe about yourself changes. And when that changes, so do your feelings and, ultimately, the choices you make in business and life in general.

Reflection Questions

Part I: Passion

1. What are some things you daydream about? What gets you excited? What do you talk about all the time?
2. Do you openly discuss your dreams/passions with others? Does hearing the dreams/passions of others stir up excitement in you? Why or why not?
3. In one sentence, what do you believe is your biggest passion in life?

Part II: God's Currency

1. What makes you feel complete? Be specific.
2. Do you believe God is a cosmic killjoy, distant ruler, genie in a bottle, or a God of unconditional love, mercy, and grace? Why?
3. Do you truly believe that God actually wants to partner with you in your daily workplace? Why or why not?

Part III: Marketplace Relationships

1. Do you find it easy making connections with people or do you have a hard time finding a point of connection with those who are different from you?
2. Why is it difficult to be authentic in business relationships?
3. In what areas of your own life have you found it difficult to be authentic?

Part IV: The Obstacle Course

1. Have any of the five "internal terrorists" (fear, judgment, pride, doubt, and lack of forgiveness) become your best friend? Why?
2. In what way is fear motivating you? What would need to change in your thinking for faith to motivate you? Be specific.
3. When you fail, how can you turn that into a positive experience?

Part V: Business Grace

1. How can a businessperson include mercy and kindness, and avoid judgment, in the workplace?
2. Do you allow the people you "love to hate" to shape you or frustrate you? Provide an example.
3. Since life is gray and not black-and-white, the business world is the same. How do you find yourself navigating the uncertainty?

Part VI: Your View of Value

1. Who determines your value?
2. Describe your purpose in life in one sentence.
3. Are rules meant to be followed exactly, or are they only a guide? Why?

Part VII: Get Rich

1. What does being rich mean to you?
2. Does giving only involve money? Explain.
3. What are some "unseen" parts of your life that give you joy? How can you incorporate these "unseens" into your daily routine? Be specific.

Part VIII: Changed

1. Are your talents gifts from God or are they man-made? Explain.
2. Have there been points in your personal life or career when you've wanted to call it quits? What kept you in the game? Be specific.
3. Change requires challenging your belief system. What one thing will you do after reading this book to change your beliefs and act on it? Describe it one sentence.